WHAT'S FUNNY ABOUT YORKSHIRE?

Books by Maurice Colbeck include:

How to be a Family Man
Queer Folk
Yorkshire Historymakers
Yorkshire: the Dales
Yorkshire Moorlands
Village Yorkshire
Made in Yorkshire

What's Funny About Yorkshire?

Maurice Colbeck

Illustrated by Anne Colbeck

Smith
Settle

First published in 1992 by

Smith Settle Ltd
Ilkley Road
Otley
West Yorkshire
LS21 3JP

ISBN Paperback 1 870071 97 2
Hardback 1 870071 98 0

British Library Cataloguing-in-Publication Data:
A catalogue record is available for this book
from the British Library.

Designed, printed and bound by
SMITH SETTLE
Ilkley Road, Otley, West Yorkshire LS21 3JP

Contents

You Won't Read This

Nobody reads introductions, which is why I haven't written one. The reason people don't read them is that they don't care how or why a book was written, they just can't wait to get stuck into it. And in the case of a book as good as this, you can't really blame 'em! I don't mind telling you, I was so keen to read it myself I could hardly wait to finish writing it.

If you are one of the people who wouldn't dream of buying a book that lacked an introduction, and you think I said I hadn't written one, that was almost certainly a printer's error. It's astonishing how many authors' mistakes turn out to be printers' errors. Authors suffer almost as much from printers' errors as politicians do from being misreported.

It's true that there is a small proportion of people who invariably do read introductions. They are the same people who always keep to the left on staircases in public buildings, who would never break rules about hospital visiting by making more than three (or is it two?) at a bed, who never walk on the grass, who invariably 'adjust their dress before leaving' and are careful always to leave everything as they themselves would wish to find it.

They are, in short, model citizens, and since there are very few of us about, the chances of one of us reading this book are extremely remote.

I mentioned errors. I'm bound to have made a few here and there but I can assure you they were all perpetrated with the best possible intentions and I hereby absolve all printers, proofreaders and editors from any blame – except where I can prove it's their fault. At the same time I apologise to my readers for mistakes made by my temperamental word processor, and for any others I find it impossible to wriggle out of. I also apologise for occasions where I might have repeated myself, on the ground that a good tale bears telling twice, and failing that, of old age.

But enough of this levity! I must, and I do, sincerely thank all who have helped me in writing this book, especially my patient (and only) wife Brenda, still sane despite years of putting up with my attacks of Author's Paranoia; Mrs Florence Garnet, daughter of the late Kit Calvert of Hawes, for allowing me to quote from her father's works; Mr P A Sherwood of the Lyke Wake Club; Mr R J Duckett of Bradford City Libraries; and fellow authors from whose works (usually referred to in the text) I've drawn inspiration.

If I have failed to give acknowledgement where it is due, or wrongly attributed the work of other writers or artists through inability to trace copyright, I tender my apologies and will endeavour to rectify the error in future editions.

Books consulted but not mentioned elsewhere in these pages include: *The Comic Postcard in English Life*, Frederick Alderson (David & Charles); *Secret Britain* (Automobile Association); *Yorkshire Cricket Greats*, John Callaghan (Sportsprint); my own *The Calendar Year* (A & C Black); *The Bradford Almanack*, Edward Hotspur Johnson (Bradford Libraries and Information Service); *Ghosts of an Ancient City*, John V Mitchell (Cerialis Press, York); *Harry Ramsden*, Don Mosey and Harry Ramsden junior (Dalesman Books); *The Haunted North Country*, C T Oxley (Dobson, Harrogate); *The Secret Life of Sooty*, Geoff Tibballs (Ringpress); *Ball of Fire*, Fred Trueman (Dent); *Phil May*, James Thorpe (Art and Technics); *Folk Tales from the North York Moors*, Peter N Walker (Hale); and *Witches in North Yorkshire*, Mary Williams (Hutton Press).

For permission to reproduce illustrations I am grateful to Bamforth & Co Ltd and Mr Arnold Taylor (pages 36 and 37); Mr Harry Ramsden junior (page 104); and Leeds City Art Galleries (pages 66 and 69).

And, of course, dear readers, I thank you too for buying or even borrowing the book. And how could you know that, if you hadn't read this introduction that I find I've written in spite of myself?

Perhaps you'd better read the rest of the book. May it give you as much fun as it's given me.

It's Nowt To Laugh At!

This, the reader will be relieved to know, is not one of those all-too-plentiful books which equate being Yorkshire with being ignorant and uncouth; whose pages abound in references to privies, fish and chip papers and funerals. No, by gum! Such volumes, let me tell you, are usually the work of authors secretly ashamed of their Yorkshire origins, who seek to ally themselves with the 'superior' South by laughing at the rest of us.

The cheek of it! Not really knowing their own native tongue, they pepper their effusions with bits of half-understood Lancashire lingo or Geordie jargon and altogether 'mek a reight mess o' t' job'.

Neither is it written by the sort of Yorkshireman who would drive anyone born outside the Broad Acres mad with rage – if he didn't kill them off with boredom first. He knows not only how many acres there are in Yorkshire, but how many square centimetres (or square centipedes, for that matter), and can't stop telling you by how many they outnumber those in other counties. He patronises Lancastrians, slanders Southerners, continually re-fights the Wars of the Roses, endlessly demands Home Rule for Yorkshire (with himself as premier no doubt), and is not above slinging his chip papers into next-door's garden if nobody's looking.

Then there's the chap who boasts endlessly about our alleged meanness, insists we've got the biggest this, the oldest that, the longest, shortest, strangest summat else and hurls incomprehensible bits of dialect at his audience as though they enshrined the wisdom of the ages.

'Get dahn i' t' cellar 'oil an' fetch up a cloompin o' gob-rollackers afore Ah gie thi a slong on t' futtock', he quotes, and expects everybody to be amazed, convulsed with mirth and devastated by their own ignorance – all at the same time. He's so overcome at finding himself a Yorkshireman, and so convinced of our breed's innate superiority (which he does his best to disprove by belonging to it), that he expects everyone else, including comers-in, off-cummed-uns and Patagonian Indians, to share his obsession.

He doesn't realise, you see, that most of those unfortunates see the counties of England as almost interchangeable and would be equally indifferent about their origins had they been born in Essex, Kent, Sussex or indeed Patagonia. Is it any wonder that they ask each other what the hecky thump he's talkin' about and quickly conclude that anyone coming from Yorkshire is certifiable?

What, then, is the distinguishing mark of the true son of the Ridings? What else but a modest dignity? We don't need to talk about our superiority, simply to demonstrate it. This book, for instance, takes Yorkshire humour seriously, as part of a prized heritage, worthy of preservation and serious study. It is not, as the ill-informed might suggest, a medium for vulgar abuse. But when its object is to tek a brussen feller down a peg ('brussen' being Yorkshire for 'busting' — with one's own importance, that is), it does so with devastating effect.

I used the masculine pronoun just now, but, sad to say, it isn't only men that are 'brussen'. Take the stuck-up would-be lady of the manor who felt that her superior status in the village required her to have the services of a maid.

She duly advertised in the local weekly and invited the most likely applicants to attend for an interview. To the first candidate, a rosy-cheeked, transparently honest country lass, the interviewer put the question:

'Have you brought your "character"?'

This flummoxed the girl for a moment or two. She had always naively believed that your character was something that went with you whether you wanted it or not: you didn't have to transport it in a brief case or a wheelbarrow.

'Mi what?', she said.

'Your character, girl', said the missus. 'If not, you'll have to get one from your former employer and come and see me again. And then, if everything else is satisfactory, I might be able to employ you.'

In due course the girl returned, empty-handed.

'Come along, girl, have you got your character or haven't you?'

'No', said the candidate, 'but Ah've gotten yours, an' Ah've just come to say Ah'm not comin'.'

Yorkshire may not have a monopoly of enlightened employers, but the county has never lacked philanthropists. Just two that spring to mind are Richard Oastler of Bradford, the 'Factory King' who battled for decent working conditions for children, and Sir Titus Salt, who built for his workers the model village of Saltaire. A farmer who hardly came into the philanthropic category used to lecture his labourers on the virtues of retiring early to bed – because, of course, such behaviour made it easier to get up early and arrive at work on time. Invariably he would conclude with the words: 'Get to bed early, lads – he was a clever feller that invented bed!'

One worker thus addressed felt he'd heard the sermon a mite too often.

''Appen so,' he said, 'but Ah know a cleverer feller.'

The farmer bristled. He was a not used to argufying with the contradictious.

'An' who's that?', he growled.

'The feller that invented dark! Cos if there were no dark there'd be no bed at thy place.'

Your true Yorkshireman is a born protester. He'd 'grum'le to be hung', as my grandmother used to say – probably about me. From Guy Fawkes (born in York) to Arthur Scargill, we seem to be in our element when we've summat to complain about. Not that we really need a grievance – we can grumble perfectly well without! For instance, you might have thought everyone would welcome a reduction in bus fares – unless you happened to live in a certain village whose inhabitants bitterly complained:

'It's all reight talkin' abaht cheaper fares, but just look how much brass we used to save bi walkin'.'

Humour, even Yorkshire humour, varies according to locality. But if it has one common feature it is a delight in 'capping', or putting in his place, the big-headed or the condescending.

R W S Bishop, a GP who recorded his experiences in a book first published in 1922 as *My Moorland Patients*, commented:

'Yorkshiremen generally are witty and humorous, but in this respect there is . . . a decided difference of degree between the moorlanders and the lowlanders. And among the moorlanders themselves, those of the Pennine Range are incomparably more witty and humorous than those of the Wolds or of the Cleveland Hills and the moorlands of north-east Yorkshire.'

He went on:

'After leaving the high moorlands I practised in the adjacent lowlands, and soon discovered that the local brand of native wit was much less pungent and sparkling than that which I had been daily accustomed to. Some of those old moorlanders could hardly open their mouths without some witty or humorous remark coming forth.'

Well, maybe! Possibly it had something to do with that sparkling moorland air. But we shouldn't generalise, as Bishop does when he says, perhaps unfairly, that the Yorkshireman's wit is 'like the man himself, of the hard-bitten variety. It is nearly always, I am afraid, provocative, wicked and even venomous.'

But it's more than mere aggression that marks the special character of Yorkshire wit, no matter where you meet with it. There's a love of nimble word-play, of parry and thrust, and a delight in making a few words say a heck of a lot.

Thus the old Yorkshire widow's retort to an over-persistent chapel deacon who was collecting for brass to mend t' chapel roof, or summat. In his private business activities, he was known to be the sort who 'would rayther nip a curran' i' two nor give a smidgin' ovverweight'. Yet he brazenly ended his appeal for funds by saying, 'You know, Mary, the Lord loveth a cheerful giver'.

"Appen so', said Mary, 'but He doesn't love a greedy takker,' and she shut the door in his face.

You patronise a moorland man at your peril, and Yorkshire youngsters never lagged far behind their elders if they thought their dignity was endangered.

Richard Blakeborough, who tells the story of the avaricious deacon, also recalls a visit to a Dales village by a school inspector who asked a local lad a question involving ribbon at so much a yard, hairpins, packets of pins and reels of thread.

'How much is that altogether? . . . Come along, boy!'

With unruffled patience, he who was thus addressed explained, 'Please sir, we're nooan lasses'.

That reminds me of a much more recent example of a visitor to a Dales village school being cut down to size. Eager to put the class at their ease, he asked them questions about their rural home-life and their parents' occupations. Whose father had a cow, he wanted to know. Whose had a bull?

'Nay', objected one young expert, 'what does tha want with a bull? T' AI [artificial insemination] feller's a sight cheaper nor onny bull!'

Perhaps local wit comes into its own most tellingly in snipings at neighbouring villages, or even in verbal sharp-shooting between one part of a village and another. 'They're all daft at t' top o' t' wood', I was once confidently assured by a villager who, of course, lived in the same village but 'at t' bottom o' t' wood'. We go further into that sort of humour in my next chapter.

But however we may fratch among oursens, we Yorkshire folk must never forget our mission – to bring light and culture to the southerners. And that's no easy task, because thanks to Peter Tinniswood and his Uncle Mort, they all think the entire North of England is composed of verdigris, impacted bunions and congealed moths.

Yet achieve it we shall, and having done that we must steel ourselves for the even more difficult task of liberating Lancashire – not forgetting Uncle Mort and his nephew Peter.

The Living Aspirin

Louis Armstrong once likened Batley to 'a living aspirin'. Whatever he meant by those mysterious words, I can testify that they were based on personal observation.

Yes indeedy! Satch was not issuing his verdict from St Louis, Missouri or Basin Street, but from Batley itself, where he had appeared on the stage of Batley's answer to the Great Pyramid, the famous Variety Club. His appearance was the biggest sensation since the visit to the town of Professor Tiplady's Bug and Flea Circus. Later, Satch toured the town, humouring an accompanying press photographer by bending down to touch the hallowed setts of the market place. It was shortly after this gesture that he made his enigmatic remark about the aspirin.

But why was Batley like an aspirin? Perhaps the famous trumpeter, whilst practising for his appearance at the Variety Club, had blown himself into a headache and had found the soothing atmosphere of the Heavy Woollen metropolis market place a balm for his pain. We must assume that the headache began before he arrived in the town, otherwise he would surely have called Batley itself a headache. And as a Batley chap myself I could never have allowed that!

We Batelians, well aware that the Romans knew our birthplace, are a proud lot, and you blacken Batley's reputation at your peril. But you can say what you like about our neighbour town Dewsbury, just as those Dewsbury folk say what they like about us. (And to any outsiders who object to that, whether from Bradford or Bratislava, I say, mind yer own b...linkin' business!)

Scores are evened and insults avenged when our respective teams knock eight bells out of each other on the rugby field at Crown Flatt or Mount Pleasant. In fact, the only real difference between the two places is that in Batley everybody invariably speaks the truth. No Batley man has ever been known to lie. And you can take my word for that.

It can only be jealousy that has inspired some of the slanderous remarks that have been made about Batley over the years. When a film was being shot in the town, based on a novel about Batley's rag trade (and I'm not talking about fashion), one of the film makers was quoted as saying Batley was 'a cemetery' (whether a living cemetery or not I don't remember).

But whatever foreigners might say, we Batley folk, besides being incorruptibly honest, are broadminded and tolerant to all outsiders (except, of course, those from Dewsbury).

Sadly, not everyone shares our tolerant nature. Love your neighbour is an admirable maxim, but it certainly doesn't seem to apply when you're talking about neighbouring towns or villages. Take Marsden, or, as they would probably retort in Huddersfield, 'No, thee tek it'.

Again, such remarks can only be inspired by that old devil jealousy, because Marsden has a lot 'going for it', as we say today. For one thing, it fringes the Peak District, which must say something about the quality of the surrounding scenery. 'Summat else to see besides mill chimneys,' Marsden folk doubtless boast. It is also the scene of such bygone engineering triumphs as the Standedge Tunnels, as well as Britain's longest canal tunnel.

In a park at Marsden you can find the table-top tomb of Enoch Taylor, famous in industrial history as the maker of the cropping frames which aroused the Luddite fury of the 'cropper lads' who feared Enoch's invention would rob them of their truly back-breaking jobs. The 'cropper lads', you see, used great pairs of shears to do the work the frames were intended to do without their help.

Now, Marsden folk aren't daft and they have a quirky sense of humour so they turned the tables on Enoch – for a time at least – by using Taylor's great hammers (also known as Enoch) to smash the hated frames. 'Enoch makes 'em, Enoch shall break 'em', was their battle cry (to which Enoch Taylor doubtless replied, 'Nay, nay lads, anybody'd think yer came from Huddersfield. When you carry on like that it's no wonder they call us Marsden Cuckoos!').

However, the epithet 'Cuckoos', hurled at Marsden folk since time immoral (as they might say in Dewsbury), had nothing to do with cropping-frames and Luddite riots, but rather more to do with natural history and the poetic impulse.

Did I tell you Marsden folk weren't green even if they were cabbage-looking? Well, it's right! They had noticed that after the arrival of the cuckoo each year the weather started to improve! Their hearts leapt with joy when they heard the first cuckoo of spring. 'It's yon bird, ageean', they'd say, smiling broadly and putting away their bedsocks an' gas blankets (electricity hadn't been invented then). 'T' weather's bahn to pick up nah. Ee, Ah doan't know what we'd do wi'out yon bird!'

But being, as I've said, a quick-witted bunch they noticed that towards the end of the summer, the cuckoo ceased to sing! After that, it wasn't long before autumn set in and then the Pennine winter in all its severity. It was a clear case of cause and effect and I'm surprised they didn't sum it up in one of those rural rhymes folk used to be so fond of:

'When cuckoo sing, he good weather bring,
When cuckoo stop, t' temperatures drop.'

You can imagine the village elders calling a meeting to decide how they could persuade 'yon bird' to stay in Marsden instead of gallivanting off to Africa as some folk said it did – 'though how they know that without follerin' it in an 'ot hair balloon Ah'm sewer Ah s'll nivver knaw!', said the chief elder.

'What we 'ev to do', said the most elderly elder, renowned for his speed at grasping difficult situations, 'is to stop it goin'!'

'We've cracked it lads, good neet', said the youngest elder, who had a date with a different kind of bird.

'How *do* we keep yon bird?', demanded a rather older elder, whose last known date had been 1066. 'Speyk, O wise one.'

The wisest and most elderly elder took his pipe from his mouth and calmly spat in the fire. 'Build a wall rahnd it, o' course', he said.

And that, according to South Pennine legend, is what they did, or tried to do, with the results that might have been predicted by wiser folk in sophisticated places like Batley.

It was probably some clever Dick in Huddersfield who first said that Marsden folk 'put t' pigs on t' wall to watch t' band go by'. Or that in Sla'wit (Slaithwaite) they 'tried to rake t' mooin aht o' t' cut' (the canal) because they were convinced it was a cheese. In the same vein of petty slander, Ossett is said to be 'wheear they blackleead t' tram lines', a charge, perhaps, of excessive civic pride that might well rebound on those levelling it.

Perhaps a lot of these gibes were inspired by envy or guilt – for instance, the charge of meanness or stupidity aimed at residents of the delightful North Riding village of Great Ayton, where Captain Cook went to school. 'Yattoners', it was said, 'wade ovver t' beck to save t' brig' (wade over the beck to save the bridge from wear).

By tradition, the village is known as 'Canny Yatton' and its inhabitants as Yattoners, though there is some disagreement as to what precisely is meant by 'canny'. The word can mean careful, mean even, but as far north as Great Ayton (which might have ended up in the so-called County of Cleveland if its people had not been determined to stay 'Yorkshire'), 'canny' can, and often does, mean pleasant or charming. Another charge levelled against Yatton, doubtless without foundation, is that its inhabitants built a fence around their village and charged visitors admission.

I'm on Yatton's side in all this! Long ago I arrived there with a photographer to prepare a major magazine feature on the village – and with only a day to gather information, pictures and all. As I wrote in an earlier book (*Village Yorkshire*), 'I found my piece almost writing itself as the love of its inhabitants for their home village carried me along like a river of pride'. They made sure I missed nothing memorable, whether it was the Postgate School (now a Captain Cook museum), where young James Cook took his first steps in education, the famous Quaker school of today, the two village greens bisected by the River Leven or Yatton's own 'mini-mountain', Roseberry Topping. They say that from its near-conical summit, young Cook would gaze over the moors to Whitby and dream about his future voyages. But the most charming of all Yatton features is its people. How they became so vilified I shall never know.

But you didn't have to live in Great Ayton to have your home town slandered. It seems that anything new, even if it was seen by the inhabitants as an improvement, would be seized upon by neighbouring townsfolk as a subject for derision. So when, in the eighteenth century, Halifax began to use bricks as well as stone for house building, someone in nearby Heptonstall penned the lines:

> 'Halifax is made o' wax,
> Heptonstall o' stone.'

It could only have been someone from Haliax who penned this addition:

> 'In Halifax there's bonny lasses
> In Heptonstall there's nooan.'

In the distant days before DDT spelt death for many parasites, Pontefract was reputed to be uncomfortably popular with small 'lodgers', hence the saying 'As sure as a louse in Pontefract'. Even fashionable Harrogate was treated with scant reverence in this rhyme:

> 'Said the devil when flying ovver 'Arrogate Wells,
> Ah think Ah'm gettin' there bi t' smells.'

Usually, however, it was the intelligence (or lack of it) in a town or village that came under attack. For instance:

> 'If you wish to find a fool
> And do it without mistake,
> Tak' t' first yer meet in Stillington,
> In Easingwold or Crayke.'

Our ancestors, it would seem, were a small-minded lot. Or perhaps it was done more in fun than in malice, as in rhymes like this, which sought to prove how important one village might be to another:

'Runswick men wi' all their toil
Come ti Steears [Staithes]
To sell their oil – '

In reply to which, the best Runswick could do was:

'Steears men, wi' all their nuts,
Come to Runswick to fill their guts.'

Supertyke

What I know of cricket (and it could be written on the pointed end of a stump) I learned from Harry East, to whom this chapter is in part a tribute. Harry was what some might call an 'original', others a 'character'. Neither word does justice to that ex-schoolmaster, part-time author, cricketer and humorist, a Yorkshireman to his toenails, but by no means your stereotypical Tyke (or stereotyke, a word I must donate to the *Oxford Dictionary* when they bring out a Yorkshire version).

Harry was extrovert, outspoken, dogmatic, xenophobic, occasionally irascible but basically kind-hearted. You could take him or let him alone. Either way, your opinion would leave him completely unmoved. As editor of *Yorkshire Life* I published his articles for years. Cricket was his favourite subject, but he could write as felicitously about ballroom dancing in the twenties and thirties or about some of the ill-starred escapades of his youth.

These often incurred penalties from Harry's father, a plumber whose temple was apparently his working men's club. When Harry's mother complained about her son's excessive patronage of the dance halls of Bradford, his dad said little, merely burnt Harry's dancing pumps.

It was probably from his dad that Harry inherited his sardonic humour and forthrightness. It was from his mother, no doubt, a chapel stalwart of unwavering zeal, that he acquired a familiarity with the lesser-known tribes of Israel which he was wont to use with good effect even in his cricket writings. Not only the Israelites, but the Amalekites, the Philistines and the Jebusites, along with their kings and prophets, were all, it seemed, waiting patiently in the everlasting pavilion to enliven Harry's anecdotes or help him make his points.

'You don't know much about cricket, do you Maurice?', Harry would say to me, in the manner of one noting a strange but harmless peculiarity. (As, for instance, he might have said: 'I 'ope you don't mind me mentioning it but Ah've noticed you've got two heads. Don't worry about it, lad – nobody's perfect'.)

From his parents, Harry had inherited a large dose of Victorianism, some might say puritanism. His god was the vengeful deity of the early evangelicals, quite capable of reacting to a much-publicised sermon by the Bishop of Durham by striking York Minster with His lightning. On the face of it, these theological convictions might appear at odds with Harry's exuberant humour; yet like all humorists, he was a serious man at heart. It was he who got me elected to the Universal Order of the Henpecked Club, and you can hardly be more serious than that. Not in my mother-in-law's opinion, anyway.

Forgive me if I've told you this story before, but it so perfectly demonstrates Harry's influence on my life that I can hardly leave it out. As members of this fraternity, it was our duty to escape (at least in theory) every Easter Monday from female domination to a secret rendezvous. Our motto: 'I serve, but not today', bore reference to our domestic labours on 364 days of the year under tyrannical wives. On the occasion that Harry sponsored my membership, he produced a tattered apron as evidence (completely spurious, need I add?) of my servitude to the sink.

It might have been a legendary link with Methodism that helped to legitimise the brotherhood in Harry's eyes. For according to some authorities, t' Enpecked (as we were called by the cognoscenti) originated about 1900 when six Methodist ministers (all presumably henpecked) met unexpectedly on an Easter Monday outing to the Halifax beauty spot called Hardcastle Crags. The six sufferers must have hit it off, because they agreed to meet again on Easter Monday the following year. Thus began the society which became a light-hearted symbol of resistance to gynocracy.

Its proceedings were supposedly secret, but the brethren knew full well that my purpose was to write about them – at no matter what peril! For as I warned on a previous occasion:

'Dire consequences are surely in store for me for divulging the secrets of this ancient brotherhood! WHY were the curtains drawn in a certain village institute before the solemn initiation of myself and three other neophytes? WHAT was the significance of the leather bag carried by the medical officer? WHY did that awesome personage need two assistants? And WHAT happened to me after I was led blindfold to an unfrequented part of the building?'

Officers of the brotherhood, I was told, included a guardian of the peace whose duty it was 'to seek out female intruders'. Perhaps 'The Women' (as they were invariably called) might be so curious and resentful about our activities as to try to infiltrate our ranks disguised as males! The notion may be less far-fetched than it sounds. Legend has it that an intrepid female reporter once tried to gain admission to our deliberations, but was excluded on the grounds that she would fail the medical.

But perhaps the best legend concerns a brother who was notoriously under the thumb of his domineering battle-axe of a missus. Somehow or other, he deluded himself that he had given her the slip. Trembling with terror, he sat in the bus that was bearing him and one or two colleagues to the appointed meeting place. There were moments when his fear of wifely retribution was so intense that he had to be restrained from leaping from the conveyance each time it slowed down.

When the bus finally halted he was almost calm – *until* he stepped from the bus to find that his termagant of a spouse had followed him by taxi.

'Ah'll 'ave nobody sayin' thar't 'enpecked – thar't not', she said, with brolly brandished, then immediately disproved that assertion by adding, 'Thar't comin' 'ome wi' me!'

My mother-in-law felt she had a similar duty in relation to me, and she never forgave me for bringing such an implied slur on her daughter and therefore on the whole family.

There were those who thought t' Enpecked was nobbut an excuse for a booze-up. They'd have been surprised by our sobriety. A pre-prandial pint at the nearest pub was permissible, but brethren who were late back for the annual meeting were frowned upon, if not bluntly reprimanded from the chair.

Besides a guardian of the peace, the officers of the society during my membership included a musical director who, they were proud to inform me, was nothing less than a Fellow of the Royal College of Organists. This truly musical fellow must have been frustrated at times, because the instrument he usually had to play was a piano. There were four hymns on the printed card which detailed procedure at our meetings, but the problem of which one to play was invariably simplified by the FRCO's admission that he 'could play 'em all except t' third'.

Some of Harry's youthful exploits might have suited the prota-gonists of TV's *Last of the Summer Wine*, but one thing he invariably took seriously – his cricket. Even so, at my instigation he wrote two light-hearted books on the sacred subject, one called *Laughter at the Wicket* and the other *Cricket is for Fun*, both of which left no room for doubt that cricket has its funny side.

I often wonder if he never felt a pang or two of guilt about these publications, because in his heart of hearts he would have agreed with George Hirst or Wilfred Rhodes or whichever titanic Tyke told some upstart Southerner:

'Up 'ere, we don't laike cricket for fun.'

As I read through what I've written I seem to hear a spectral voice, unquestionably Harry's, complaining, 'Yer keep sayin' yer goin' to write about cricket, but yer takin' a hell of a long time to get round to it!'

And so, by special request, my next chapter will be about cricket. And since, as Harry would certainly agree, I really know nowt about it, I shall concentrate on its funny side.

What's Funny About Cricket?

We may not 'laike cricket for fun' in Yorkshire, but cricket truly has its funny side, or where – to name but one – did Johnny Wardle come from?

A A Thomson, whom someone called 'the happiest of cricket writers' and who, like Harry, was a contributor to *Yorkshire Life*, used to say that Wardle was a born clown in his mastery of mime and quick gesture. If a demon 'bodyline' bowler caught Johnny a painful knock on the right shoulder, he would energetically rub his left leg; a knock on the left breast apparently produced agony in the right buttock. After making an impossible catch, Johnny might deftly secrete the ball in his pocket then dash for the boundary as if his life depended on stopping some mightily-swiped ball that only he could see. Or he might just as confidently toss an imaginary catch into the air, to the accompaniment of cheers, while the real ball was speeding to the boundary.

Returning to the pavilion after his stumps had been unquestionably skittled, he might confront the spectators with a puzzled frown. 'Did it look out from here?', he would ask, convulsing his audience while remaining utterly straight-faced himself.

Johnny may have been the sort of person whose sense of humour got in the way of his advancement. It often happens. Jokers arouse discomfort in those lacking a sensitive funny-bone, and all too many people confuse reliability with solemnity. Once, interviewing the late Sir William Worsley, a figure of great consequence in the annals of the county club, I ventured to wonder if Wardle had not been harshly dealt with.

'I think he'll be all right in league cricket,' replied Sir William politely, in a tone that suggested the subject was closed. I was out of my depth and knew it, so left it at that.

Johnny Wardle played in the big league, which Harry East viewed with a certain cynicism.

'Cricket', he wrote, in the thunderous Victorian style he reserved for really serious matters like Armageddon, the Last Judgement or a derby match between Bingley and Spen, 'was neither born nor succoured on the mighty Test Match grounds . . . But it is there cricket will die unless the common man . . . asserts himself and annihilates the hydra-headed dragon of sponsorship, flood-lit abominations, yellow pads, crimson umpires' coats, Sunday afternoon's tawdry caricature and the tarnishing of a noble game to the whims of those who would defile its purity for greed and gold.'

That should put the ungodly in their place.

Harry despised both the hypocrites and the money-grubbers, who, as he might have said, wearing his Biblical prophet's hat, tried to turn the temple of cricket into a den of robbers. But the honest scallywag for whom cricket, no matter how rarefied the setting, remained nobbut a game, inspired his heartfelt affection. Such a man was Tom Emmett, 'Clown Prince of Cricket', the Halifax-born professional captain of Yorkshire for five seasons before he handed over in 1883 to the young patrician, Martin (later Lord) Hawke. That worthy took command at a time when Yorkshire had gained a reputation for fielding – execrably!

'What's the team like, Tom?', asked the ambitious new captain, with a serious air that did nothing to intimidate Emmett. Tom shook his head in the manner of one about to impart bad news. 'Well, Mr 'Awke', he said, 'Ah'm afraid this team's in t' grip of a hepidemic. But don't worry', he added, as alarm dawned on his new captain's face, '*it's not catchin'*.'

I have mentioned Wardle. Those old enough to have seen an earlier joker, Cecil Parkin, might well feel that there must be something in reincarnation. For Johnny, had he been born a bit later, might have been thought to have inherited some of his great predecessor's antics. Yet while Wardle was unquestionably entitled by birth to a place in the Yorkshire side, there was enough doubt about Parkin's qualifications to bring his Yorkshire career to an end after only one season.

Cecil was born in Eaglescliffe, which apparently rendered his eligibility a near thing. He was later to claim that if his bed had been placed at the southern instead of the northern end of his bedroom, Lord Hawke would never have had to relinquish him to Lancashire.

Parkin (according to A A Thomson, who included him in his collection of *Odd Men In*) was supreme as a slow bowler in making batsmen look complete idiots. They would step first of all forward and then back to one of Cecil's specials (which they invariably missed), then stand apparently mesmerised by the ball as it wound about their legs like a playful kitten before demolishing their stumps in anything but a kittenish fashion. Faced with such a bowler, says Thomson with manifest sympathy, the batsman appeared to be playing cricket on skates while defending his wicket with an umbrella.

Parkin's conjuring tricks extended to more than his bowling. On a voyage with the England side to Australia, he frequently entertained his fellow passengers with his sleight of hand and a tongue that was equally dextrous. All the players had been seasick in the Bay of Biscay except one, who, Cecil opined, was 'too mean to part with owt'.

But if he could take a rise out of his team mates, Cecil was at times quite gullible himself − or allowed others to think he was. He apparently believed it when told that in equatorial realms he would feel the bump of the ship crossing the Line; and that if he didn't keep his cabin porthole closed all the way through the Red Sea, the flying fishes would whizz in and attack him. In such cases it is difficult to decide quite who was taking a rise out of whom.

Once, when Lord Tennyson (grandson of the poet) was captain of the England Test side of 1921, 'Horseshoe' Collins had stood at the wicket for almost six hours, during which time he had scored forty. To say the Old Trafford crowd was restless is more than an understatement. Finally, one spectator could bear it no longer and called to the captain:

'Hey, Tennyson, read him some o' thi Grandad's poems.'

'He 'as done,' retorted Parkin with less than a split second's pause for thought. 'The beggar's been asleep for hours.'

Harry East considered Kumar Shri Ranjitsinhji (hereinafter referred to as Ranji) 'one of the four greatest batsmen'. Other commentators have called him a genius, as well as a rogue and a sycophant. But whatever his failings might have been, Ranji had that most redeeming of features, an unquenchable sense of humour.

He demonstrated this risible faculty most effectively after performing in a match at Bridlington in 1842. Some of the credit, or discredit, for what follows must go to Ranji's team-mates in the England side who convinced the local Tykes that Ranji, reputed heir to an Indian princedom, could not speak a word of English.

Yorkshiremen are often not above taking a rise out of a stranger −

and few appeared stranger than Ranji, identifiable, declared his colleagues, not only by his colour and a dashing moustache, but by the impeccable quality of his cream silk shirts, invariably buttoned to the wrist.

Convinced that Ranji could not understand a word they said, the fielders indulged the full power of their ribald talent on this visiting oriental. As he serenely batted on, his mockers vied with each other in the offensiveness of their jibes. Still Ranji continued to bat.

When he reached fifty the jokes were becoming rather laboured. At a hundred, the detractors' tones had an edge of desperation. And still Ranji batted on, clearly heading for another hundred at least.

Only when his score stood at 142 and success was beginning to pall did he allow himself to be ousted from the crease. Perhaps he was bored, perhaps he was tired, but he had certainly recovered sufficiently to attend a dinner that same evening, and make a speech in impeccable English, just the speech you would expect from a man educated at first in the hands of expensive private tutors and, after that, at Cambridge University.

Ranji may have been more subtle than the average cricket humorist, but cricket has never lacked for clowns. One who was given that appellation, though he hardly deserved it, was Emmott Robinson. For 'no more humourless cricketer', Harry East told me, 'ever walked the face of the earth'.

Coming upon Emmott one day in his later years, Harry spotted him, where he was often to be found, in the reading room of the mechanics institute, Bradford. When Harry saw Emmott take a pill from a little bottle in his waistcoat pocket, he asked anxiously about his health. Harry's fears were justified: all was from well in that department and apparently it was 'all Wilfred's fault'.

Need I tell you that Wilfred was Wilfred Rhodes, who was as famous for the strength of his own stomach as he was for his bowling? Wilfred frequently spent periods as cricket coach to some Indian maharajah and would prevail upon the hapless Emmott to accompany him on these jaunts. As thrifty Yorkshiremen, the two would live in a corner of the pavilion, shopping for their own food, on expeditions which sometimes took Wilfred to the cheap village market they had been warned to avoid. It had been one of Wilfred's bargains, a chicken, which Emmott blamed for his 'stomach'.

It had 'nivver been reight since', he said, and had left its owner with a distinctly unfavourable view of the Subcontinent. When he came home to Bradford, Emmott 'never wanted to see another Indian' and was less than enchanted to find that since that day 'they've come to live all round me'.

Freddie Trueman is too formidable to be summed up as merely a joker. He is a sportsman of enormous stature and every ounce a Yorkshireman. Such a character can hardly escape being seized upon by the media and transformed into a grotesque travesty of his real self.

This, of course, is often the price of fame, and though Freddie is big enough to rise above all the bunkum that used to be written and spoken about him, I can understand why he seized the opportunity to do a bit of debunking on his own account in his autobiography, *Ball of Fire*. Take the so-called Gunga Din incident, which, as Freddie pointed out, probably did him more harm than any of the other stories that circulated about him.

It was alleged that during a dinner party given in honour of the 1952 Indian tourists by their high commissioner, Freddie, seated at the top of the table, nudged a high-ranking Indian diplomat in the ribs and said, 'Hey, Gunga Din, pass t' salt'. Such fables are easy to spread and all too difficult to destroy, despite Freddie's convincing demonstration of the absurdity of such a story: he is supposed to have uttered the famous words while seated at the top table and they would never', commented Fred, 'have seated England's most junior cap in such an exalted position . . . Stories like that made me more than ever a prime target for the press boys who were always probing for a bit more scandal about Fred'.

I can understand Fred's exasperation, but 'scandal' is not really the word to describe a story like that. What the press boys were after (and who can blame them?) was the delightful, colourful, down-to-earth, honest and humorous Fred himself.

So I believe him when he says that most of the best-circulated stories about him allege actions supposedly performed when he was miles away – at Bristol, say, when he was in fact at Lord's, or at Lord's when the world knew perfectly well that he was in Brighton.

Uncle Ephraim and the Mermaids

As a little lad, I found it fairly easy to believe that Uncle Ephraim had fought with Nelson at Trafalgar, though my credulity may have been a little strained by the news that he'd helped King Alfred put the Danes in their place. But then, why should a mere shaver like me question his version of history? With his bristling white moustache, beetling eyebrows and craggy features, my great-uncle looked to me at least as old as Penyghent.

Anyway, they don't tell lies in heaven, and heaven, for me, was Uncle Ephraim's hen-run, where he spent most of his life, whatever the weather or time of year. In winter he wore his threadbare old army greatcoat, the pockets of which were an apparently bottomless source of 'spice' – I mean real Yorkshire spice – Pontefract cakes and aniseed balls and Poor Bens, my favourites, especially if they came with a dusting of the coal-dust, cement or fertiliser which found a permanent home in Uncle Ephraim's pockets.

But although I was delighted to be in his presence, and especially so in his hen-run, I found it increasingly difficult, as my years increased, to credit his yarns. On the day he told me that he had gone to school with Friar Tuck I could contain my doubts no longer.

'Yer kiddin' me, aren't you, Uncle Ephraim?', I said, sadly.

It was the first time I had questioned his veracity, and instantly I was flooded with guilt and horror.

'Aren't yer?', I faltered.

He looked at me just once, then strode out of the hen-run so fast that my short legs had no chance to keep up. I trailed after him, kicking out my misery against every stone in the road, and vowed never to doubt Uncle Ephraim's word again.

The next time we met, his gap-toothed smile seemed as gentle as ever. I could tell he was just as anxious as I was to restore diplomatic relations.

'I went to Filey last week wi' t' school trip', I told him. ''Ave you been to Filey, Uncle Ephraim?'

'I went to Filey', he pronounced weightily, 'when t' dragon wor theer.'

'What dragon?'

He gave me a pitying glance.

'They don' t tell yer nothin' at school these days, do they?'

'No, Uncle Ephraim.'

'Yer've 'eard o' Filey Brigg, Ah reckon?'

I nodded. 'It's a gurt lump o' rock juttin' aht into t' sea.'

'Well, that's summat,' he grunted. 'But Ah'll bet you've nivver 'eard o' Billy Biter . . . Billy was a tailor, t' most 'enpecked feller 'at ever lived i' Filey.'

'What's "enpecked" Uncle Ephraim?'

'Tha'll learn,' he said with a sigh. 'But don't interrupt, or Ah'll tell thi nowt no more. Nah, Billy wor partial to parkin, and one night 'e were walkin' 'ome, munchin' a piece o' sticky parkin and wonderin' what job his missus 'ud 'ave waitin' for him, when 'e fell into a gully near where Filey Brigg is today. In this gully there lived a dragon – an' if tha axes me what a dragon is Ah'll gie thi a clip on t' lug. This dragon snapped up Billy's parkin, an' it wor that suited wi' it, it wanted some more. So –'

'Uncle Ephraim –'

'What nah?'

'Why didn't it eat Billy?'

'"Appen it would have, if a daft little lad 'adn't kept askin' it questions, but just then it wanted some more parkin. Onnyroad, Billy realised that as long as t' dragon were gettin' parkin it wouldn't eyt 'im, so 'e called to his wife tellin' 'er what 'ad 'appened and axin' her to bake some more. Well, shoo grumbled and moaned, but she didn't want to loise Billy, or she'd 'ave nobody else to 'enpeck, so she got t' oven goin' and set abaht makkin' more parkin.

'"Make it a rahnd 'un this time", shouts Billy, who 'ad a reight good 'ead on 'is shoulders, an' wanted to keep it there.

'"What for?", says his wife.

'"Just do it", says Billy.

'"Round parkin? Ah niver 'eard owt so daft", says 'is wife, just like a woman.

'Billy's idea, yer see, was to mek t' parkin rahnd so's his wife could roll it into t' gully without comin' too near t' dragon, in case shoo got etten. But yer know what wimmin are. Well, I expect yer sooin will.

'Onnyroad, Billy's wife wor as stubborn as any other woman. She wasn't bahn to let any dragon freeten 'er! Wi' a gurt slab o' parkin – square parkin – in her airms she walked up to t' gully.

'"Coom on doggie", she says, 'oddin' it aht in front of 'er.

'T' dragon turned his 'een off Billy and gave 'er a long look.

'"Nice doggie", says Billy's wife, "coom an' eat yer parkin".

'T' dragon wor a bit ponderous and slow-movin' like, on account of his size.

"'Coom on for yer parkin, doggie", says Billy's wife. "Ah shan't tell yer no more . . ."

'Shoo niver spok' a truer word, 'cos t' dragon took t' parkin an' Billy's wife with it and swallowed t' lot with 'ardly a gulp. Nah, eytin' Billy's wife wouldn't 'ave 'armed it – a bit of indigestion 'appen, but nowt worse – it were t' parkin 'at caused t' bother.

'Well, work it aht for thisen . . . Tha knaws what real fresh-baked Yorkshire parkin's like.'

'Sticky', I said.

'Tha's hit it. T' dragon chomped it up wi' great enjoyment but then it couldn't 'oppen its mouth – t' parkin had glued its jaws together! It tried all roads to get 'em loise, but could it 'eck!

'So it went dahn to t' sea to try an' wash its teeth clean. But t' cowd watter made that parkin in its gob set as hard as concrete.'

'So what 'appened?'

'It starved to deeath o' course', said Uncle Ephraim.

'An' what folk today call Filey Brigg is nowt but that dragon's bones, a bit fossilised an' that, wi' barnacles and limpets stuck on 'em, but bones nevertheless.'

'What about Billy?'

''E shed a few tears o' course at t' funeral, being a soft-hearted, decent sort o' chap. But nobody nivver called 'im 'enpecked no more.'

'Did you go to t' funeral, Uncle Ephraim?'

'Course Ah did. We 'ad elderberry wine and t' parkin Billy's wife 'ad made – afore she deed, tha understands. Well, there were no sense i' wastin' it.'

'Are yer sure abaht – abaht t'parkin?', I asked him.

'Of course Ah'm sure.'

He fished deep in his greatcoat pocket and produced a small piece of parkin that looked as truly fossilised as anything Filey Brigg could offer.

'It's a bit dry now, o' course, but – '

I accepted it, chewed it with relish and swallowed it – just as I swallowed all Uncle Ephraim's offerings – without further question.

'We're goin' to Scarborough wi' t' Sunday school, Uncle Ephraim', I said the next time we met.

He looked up from his perch, an upturned bucket in the middle of his hen-run.

'Yer mun watch out for t' mermaids', he said.

I studied his lugubrious features, but there was no hint of a smile.

'There i'nt no . . . mermaids?'

The words faded out along with my scornful confidence, because you never knew with Uncle Ephraim.

'Isn't there?', he asked, his eyes fixed on a white wyandotte in the middle distance. He transferred his gaze to the one-legged khaki campbell duck which swam in a lop-sided fashion round the old tin bath that did duty as a duckpond.

'An' – an' Ah once went into t' aquarium at Blackpool Tower an' there were all sorts o' fish in there but Ah didn't see any mermaids theer either.'

'Didn't yer?', he enquired politely and lapsed once more into silence. He knew those silences had to be filled by a question from me – no matter how hard I strove to be silent.

'Did *you* ever see a mermaid, Uncle Ephraim?', I said. I had walked into the trap yet again.

'How could Ah?', he replied. 'Tha's just said there i'nt no mermaids.'

'Not at Scarborough, onnyroad.'

He looked sorrowfully at me for some seconds. Then:

'Ah niver said there wor. Ah just telled thi to look aht for 'em 'cos tha were goin' to t' seaside. There's other places than Scarborough. An' Ah niver said Ah'd seen a mermaid – not a mermaid exactly. But Ah can tell thee what Ah did see. Shall Ah tell thi or not?'

'Aye, go on then.'

My ungraciousness brought a glint to his eye, but failed to deter him. Truth was (if truth came into it) that he wanted to tell the story as much as I wanted to hear it.

'It wor at Skinningrove – '

'Wheer's that?'

'In Yorkshire, o' course, but some fowk 'at owt to know better calls it Cleveland as if it were summat different fra' Yorkshire. Cleveland means Cliffland, tha knaws, an' the real Cleveland 'as allus been part o' Yorkshire.'

'An' what wor you doin' theer?'

'Oh, Ah forget – it wor a long time sin'. 'Appen I wor a fisherman, or mebbe I 'ad a job in t' iron works theer, if they were theer then.'

Somehow this sounded more convincing than detailed recollection might have been. It seemed natural enough that Uncle Ephraim, who had lived so long and done so much, should occasionally have difficulty remembering precisely where he was at any given time.

'Skinningrove wor nobbut a fishin' village then. There were a bay theer, an' high cliffs – Ah told thee them parts used to be called "Cliffland" . . . '

'An' they 'ad a mermaid', I prompted.

'No', he replied, oblivious of my impatience. 'Ah nivver said they 'ad a mermaid . . . It wor a mer*man*.'

He regarded me with triumph.

'It wor t' fishermen that brought 'im in. They copped 'im in their nets one day an' wondered what the 'ummer he was. My mate, who was t' skipper o' t' boat, actually asked 'im, official like: "What's thi name and wheer art tha bahnd for, and what art tha doin' tryin' to swamp my boat, the *Cleveland Maid*, out o' Skinningrove?"'

'E were an eddicated lad, were t' skipper, so 'e tried 'im with a bit of French, callin' 'im monsewer, but that nobbut seemed to upset him, for he sort o' screeched at 'im. 'Appen he felt insulted like, bein' talked at in French, an' 'im probably a Yorkshire merman.'

'What did 'e look like?'

Conveniently, Uncle Ephraim found it 'a bit 'ard to picture 'im after all this time. But Ah know 'e ate fish – they could 'ardly fill 'im.'

' 'Opin' no doubt to finnd out summat abaht 'im, they put im in an old tummle-down 'ouse near t' beach, and fowk came from far an' near to gawp at him.

'There were some as said 'e was t' devil and another feller said he wor King Neptune an' we owt to let 'im go or we'd 'appen be invaded by an army o' mermen. But t' others said 'e wor King Neptune's spy an' if we let 'im go 'e'd go an' tell Neptune wheer Skinningrove wor an' then t' mermen 'ud coom an' pinch all t' women an' tak' 'em away under t' sea.

'There were one young woman used to come an see 'im every day and they used to look at one another for 'awf an hour at a time, almost as if they were in love. 'E were allus fair suited to see 'er, or any young woman come to that. But 'e seemed partickler fond o' that one 'at came every day.

'Some fowk thowt it wor a reight good joke. "When are you two bahn to get wed?", they'd say. "An' will yo' live on t' land or in t' watter? An' will yer 'ave bairns or tadpoles?"

'But she took no notice, an' nowt they said seemed to bother t' merman awther.

'Ah doan't know what would 'ave happened in t' finish, nobbut one day t' merman took 'is 'ook.'

'Yer mean 'e went fishin'?'

'No, yer cawf-eead. I mean he 'opped it, did a bunk. What do they teych yer at schooil these days?'

'Nowt abaht mermaids', I said.

'E wor last seen in t' sea wi' 'is top 'awf pokin' aboon t' waves and bobbin' up an' down as if 'e wor bowin' like, an thankin' 'em for lookin' after 'im so weel. An' t' young woman 'at 'ad ta'en such a fancy to 'im wor stood on t' sands skrikin' 'er eyes out, but it didn't fetch 'im back. He dived into t' watter ageean. And they saw 'im no more!'

Uncle Ephraim paused for a moment to savour the full dramatic impact of his words. Then he said, 'So don't forget to look out for mermaids when tha goes to Scarborough.'

There was a hint of challenge in his voice. Recklessly I took it up.

'But that were a mer*man*. There were nowt in that tale abaht mermaids . . . An' Ah'm off to Scarborough, not Skinningrove!'

He bristled with fury.

'Ah'll tell thi nowt no more! Ah said tha were a cawf'eead an' tha'rt doin' thi' best to prove it. If there's mermen it stands to reason there must be merwomen, or there wouldn't be nobody to be mothers to t' merbairns, an' their entire race 'ud dee aht.'

'Ah reckon they must 'ave, cos Ah've nivver seen ony', I said.

Uncle Ephraim appeared not to have heard. His eyes were fixed on a prowling cat at the far end of the hen-run. Suddenly he snatched up a bit of slate and hurled it at the feline, which yowled and fled the premises.

'We didn't see no mermaids at Scarborough', I told him happily, the next time we met.

''Appen tha should be goin' to Steears instead', said Uncle Ephraim.

''Ow do yer spell it?' I said. An' doan't say "I-T".'

'S-T-A-I-T-H-E-S. But them as lives theer calls it Steears', he explained with infinite condescension.

He handed me a peace-offering of a dust-coated scrap of pink and white rock from the pocket of his greatcoat and waited for my inevitable questions.

'Is there mermaids at Staithes – Steears?'

His gap-toothed smile betokened satisfaction and he responded promptly to his cue.

'It's a grand little place is Steears', he began. 'Tha goes dahn a reight steep 'ill an' cooms to a bay and ther's little cottages 'at looks as if they're bahn to drop off t' cliffsides into t' watter. There were once a whole row of 'em swept away. An' there's a pub called the Cod an' Lobster on t' edge o' t' harbour. Doan't ask me 'ow it doesn't get weshed into t'sea . . . Tha's 'eard of Captain Cook?'

'Course I 'ave.'

'So they do teych yer summat at schooil these days! Well, Captain Cook, when 'e was a lad, worked in a shop at Steears.'

'Did you know him?'

He ignored my mischievous question.

'An' t' wimmin still wear t' owd frilly bonnets now an' then, called Steears bonnets', he went on.

I was beginning to weary of the travelogue.

'Does t' mermaids wear 'em?', I asked him.

'Wear what?'

'These frilly bonnets?'

He looked at me severely. I half-expected him to demand the return of his half-sucked scrap of rock, so swallowed it quickly.

'There were these two mermaids', said Uncle Ephraim, 'weshed ashore at Steears durin' a terrible storm. Beautiful lasses they were', he went on, 'wi' long, golden 'air an' scaly tails like fish. I s'all niver forget 'em . . . '

'What year was this?'

'It wor affoar you were born', Uncle Ephraim replied crushingly. ' 'Ave Ah to go on wi' t' tale or 'aven't Ah? Ah've a good mind to tell thi nowt no more!'

I nodded.

'These two mermaids were that exhausted after battlin' wi' t' waves they fell fast asleep as sooin as they landed on t' sands an' didn't wakken up till next mornin', when they fun' theirsens surrounded bi a crowd o' gawpin' Steearsers –that's Steears folk.

'T' mermaids were reight freetened and tried to wriggle their way back to t' watter. But t' tide wor too far out an' before they knew where they wor they'd been grabbed bi t' village fowk and pushed into t' lock-up wi' nowt but a couple o' handfuls o' raw fish to eyt. Naturally they felt out o' their element an' they pleaded to be ta'en back to t' watter.

'But t' Steearsers couldn't mak' 'ead nor tail of owt they said and the more t' mermaids pleaded, the angrier t' village folk became. So after a bit they cahred quiet. But it wor a miserable life for t' poor lasses wi' t' village fowk chuckin' stones at 'em an' t' lads gawpin at 'em.'

'What did you do, Uncle Ephraim?'

'I hobserved', he replied loftily. 'As time went by, t' sea-lasses picked up a few words o' Steears talk an' t' Steearsers managed to leearn a bit o' t' mermaids' language. It wor a village o' simple, rough fisherfolk, but try as they might they couldn't 'elp but tak' to theeas two grand lasses 'oo niver 'ad a wrong word to say to nobody, no matter what they had to put up wi' . . .'

He heaved a deep sigh.

'Ah reckon yer must 'a' been in love wi' one on 'em yersen – 'appen wi' both on 'em', I said.

'There's no charge for reckonin'', said Uncle Ephraim. 'Now shut up and listen. One day t' lasses were laikin' in a rock pool on t' sands an t' Steears folk weren't takin' much notice. So when t' next big wave rolled in, they made a dash for t' watter, wrigglin' their tails like billyo. Affoar t' Steearsers knew it, t' mermaids were in t' watter, divin' an' swimmin' about like a pair o' dolphins, they were that suited to be back wheer they belonged.

'All t' Steearsers could do wor shout abuse at 'em, an' that seemed to put t' mermaids' backs up. One on 'em stood up on her tail and gave t' village a reight lambastin'. She didn't awf tell 'em their name. An' to rahnd it off, she called dahn a curse on 'em:

'"The sea", she said, "shall flow to Jackdaws Well!"'

'Them Steearsers did nowt but laugh at that, 'cos Jackdaws Well wor a long chalk fra' t' sea. Onnyroad up, t' sea kept on nibblin' at Steears, as it still does to this day. Sure enough, t' time came when it flowed to Jackdaws Well, an' even weshed it away. What do yer think o' that?'

'Ah wor just wonderin'', Ah said, "ow long is a mermaid's tail?'

'Sahnds a bit of a daft question to me', said Uncle Ephraim. 'It depends on t' size o' t' mermaid o' course. Why does tha want to knaw?'

'Ah were nobbut thinkin' 'at *thy* tale were gettin' a bit on t' long side.'

'Ah'll tell thi nowt no more', he shouted after me as I ran out of the hen-run.

'Is that a promise?', I yelled back.

The little splinter of slate he threw after me caught me stingingly on the back of the neck.

What a Card!

What sort of a man makes a name for himself as a comic postcard artist? His specialities include honeymoon couples in bed, hugely pregnant females, inadequate husbands and above all – bosoms, and more bosoms.

All the 'boobs', as they are strangely termed today, have been drawn with what I can best call affection, and so have the girls themselves. Their faces display innocence or astonishment, occasionally exasperation or shock. They are clearly *nice* girls, whose reactions to imagined impropriety or embarrassing situations appear dated in relation to their cute good looks and revealing costumes. Generally, they're the sort of girls you'd take home to Mum if only you could trust Dad.

Nobody could call these drawings obscene. (Or could they? Some of the censorship committees in seaside towns have been known to manifest rather strange sensibilities.) Nor could they be called pornographic. Vulgar? Yes, if you mean the vulgarity that goes with sea breezes, sticks of rock, candy floss and consumable false teeth. But for me the distinguishing mark of Arnold Taylor's work is a kind of light-hearted comic eroticism. Here, you feel, is a man who *likes* women. Even the heavily pregnant girl who realises, too late, that 'I should have danced all night', is drawn with sympathy.

And even Arnold's fat seaside ladies are 'ladies'. Comic, maybe, but not ugly and certainly not drawn like some cards I've seen, by a misogynist. But then it's not surprising that Arnold Taylor draws 'ladies', since he is himself that nice old-fashioned thing, a gentleman.

Sex, he acknowledges, 'comes into the cards', but not in a nasty or furtive way. 'Gee, Fred – I didn't know we could have so much fun without laughing', says a bride in bed with her new husband. There's no date on the card, but the sentiment seems to belong to an earlier era.

I met Arnold, for the second time in twenty years, outside the

Holmfirth Postcard Museum. A slight, soldierly man, still straight-backed, he looks a classic example of the Eighth Army veteran. Wounded in the North African desert, promoted to sergeant, he was robbed of an eventual commission only by the outbreak of peace.

Due to the influence of his colonel, an amateur artist, Arnold was transferred to Army public relations. He prizes among other watercolours a painting of a desert camel race organised by his colonel.

Holmfirth, capital of the comic postcard kingdom which Arnold entered as a school-leaver aged fourteen, has been a funny place for longer than anyone can remember. And the humour has rarely been of the subtlest. The risible tradition might have started with the silent slapstick films made there by Bamforths around 1900, which starred local folk like Fred ('Shiner') Beaumont, so nicknamed because he was a french polisher by trade, or Freddie Bullock.

'I knew Freddie Bullock', said Arnold, with a hint of pride.

Justifiable pride, for Freddie Bullock, even if he didn't know it, played a seminal part in the birth of the cinema – that is, along with Shiner Beaumont, his 'sparring partner'. I use that metaphor with good reason, for a crafty producer knew well how to lure the two into battle. He would instruct each of his two stars separately on *his* particular part in the plot. Each was given the impression that his was the dominant role and each, ignoring the protests of the opposition, would strive to carry out his instructions to the letter.

So, when the script required Freddie Bullock and Shiner to have a stand-up fight in a boat on the lake at Honley Pleasure Gardens, each contestant entered the fray convinced that he was the one whose job it was to throw the other into the water. The result, while it represented the very height of frustration for the protagonists, provided the most hilarious footage.

Film-making ended at Holmfirth in 1914, killed off perhaps by the outbreak of World War One. Now Bamforths embarked in a big way on the production of sentimental cards to send to your man at the Front. But in the bleak postwar years, sentiment went out of fashion, and comedy cards became the order of the day.

Women, it might be argued by feminists, are often the butt of the humour we have seen in more recent times. If they aren't being shot off a lavatory seat by a new-fangled machine operated by the 'Super Drain Flush Co' (a purely imaginary organisation, need I point out?), they're yelling 'Rape' after driving an open sports car into a nude

male statue that has consequently broken off at the knees and toppled on top of the car and driver. Or they're in police uniform confronting a drunk. 'Anything you say will be taken down', warns the WPC. The retort 'Knickers' is so predictable that I hardly need to quote it. Had the policewoman smiled as if she shared the joke, perhaps the feminists would have less of a case, but of course she looks furious, which is meant to add to the fun.

On the whole, however, the jokes could hardly be called sexist, though the purely sexless ones are not really so funny. Two men meet in mid-air, one in flying gear descending from a falling plane, the other a workman rising from an explosion on the ground.

'Do you know anything about parachutes?', asks the falling flyer.

'No mate – I don't even know about gas ovens', says the ascending artisan.

'What are you doing, Dad?' a small boy asks his father, as pyjama-clad they kneel at each side of the bed in attitudes of prayer.

'Same as you, son', says the father.

'I shouldn't, Dad', warns his offspring, 'There isn't one on that side.'

One card shows a large and a small man sharing the shower, while the small man makes some heartfelt comment about 'equality'.

So men, especially fathers, are fair game too, but usually not so much *because* they're men, whereas the jokes about women depend to a large extent on gender.

Holmfirth is now known to the world as the setting for *Last of the Summer Wine*, a television comedy series which has won a remarkable degree of acceptance far beyond its Pennine place of origin. Characters like the ragamuffin Compo or Norah Battye, she of the wrinkled stockings, can hardly be considered Holmfirth stereotypes, but they have something in common with the broad humour of the place, which surely influenced the young Arnold Taylor when he embarked on his comical calling.

Modestly, Arnold attributes his entry into the art world largely to the fact that 'I wasn't very good at maths, but I was rather good at drawing'.

He had had no training in art, but at Bamforths he worked with 'Mr Tempest', as he still respectfully calls Douglas Tempest, who had joined the firm in 1911 and stayed with them until the early 1950s. Tempest, who lived through the tennis craze of the comparatively innocent twenties, made great play with terms like 'courts', 'rackets' and 'love all'. Early flying exploits also brought on attacks of punning – with talk about 'getting the wind up coming down'. Motoring, too: 'What's a pedestrian, Dad?', asks the small passenger in his father's saloon. 'I'll show you, my boy', says Father. 'We should run across one pretty soon.'

Mr Tempest seems to have taken young Arnold under his wing after Frank Bamforth had spotted talent in his spare-time doodlings while officially at work in the photographic department. Arnold did his first stint as an art student (two days a week at first, then evening classes) at Huddersfield while continuing to work at Bamforths.

His earlier comic card efforts were largely concerned with seaside fat ladies – 'because in those days, people used to go to the seaside for a week and would buy at least a couple of dozen postcards to send to relatives or friends at the factory or the pub. That was probably when the postcard business was at its peak.'

Bamforths had to submit their designs to a censorship committee at Blackpool. Such committees, like committees everywhere, sometimes seemed to work in mysterious ways, not least in what they rejected.

Some postcard committees have imposed bans on subjects as disparate as drugs, angels, the national flag sewn on knickers, prostitutes, beds or nuns. One of Bamforth's rejected designs showed a couple in bed – nothing unusual in that, nor, perhaps about the fact that the wife fears her husband's passions are somewhat cooler than once they were. 'Why', she complains, 'don't you bite my ear in bed like you used to?' 'I can't', replies her spouse, not unreasonably, 'my teeth are in the bathroom.'

Such committees usually included members of the wholesale and retail trades involved in the sale of postcards, a clergyman, a lawyer or two, and members of various women's organisations. When you consider how many family and other sensibilities might inhibit the committee members' judgement, it might be considered a miracle that any cards at all got past the censor. However, some firms (Bamforths included), while submitting their designs to the censorship committees, kept a watchful eye themselves on their products. Thus designs which had been approved by the committee were sometimes scrapped by the company itself, if, on second thoughts, they were considered 'a bit near the knuckle'.

Over the years, says Arnold, censorship standards have relaxed.

'Nowadays it's mostly sex. A lot of firms that came in and went out quickly, produced what I call rubbish. We kept going because our artwork was better. Because you've got to have humour in the drawing as well as in the caption. Sex-centred humour', believes Arnold, whether on comic cards or in television comedy, 'may be going out of fashion because it can't go any further, and, in short, because it is no longer funny.'

Nobody meeting Arnold for the first time would guess his former occupation. They would certainly not be immediately convulsed with mirth. During my conversation with him I think he laughed only once. It was when I asked him: 'Are you a jokey man?' That produced a brief chuckle. 'I'm a humorous man, I believe', he said thoughtfully, 'but I can't tell a joke. In the middle of it I forget the punch-line.'

But the real expert in any field rarely looks or acts the part. When

Arnold met Donald McGill, perhaps his most famous predecessor, he thought he looked more like 'a little solicitor' than whatever might be the popular idea of the comic artist.

After leaving the Army, Arnold spent some time freelancing in London. Then Derek Bamforth, grandson of the founder of the firm (who once admitted to me that he never sent holiday postcards), asked him to return to Holmfirth. Arnold was not sorry to accept the invitation. While it was not essential that as a freelance he should live in London, it was certainly more convenient.

'But I couldn't think of living in a city for ever. I'm a countryman', he says.

If he had his life to live over again, would he choose a different course? He thinks for a moment, then says, yes, he very well might. Notwithstanding his comic flair, he is a serious artist whose talent is obvious and it seemed clear that he felt this was a side of his nature which could have found greater fulfilment.

On the other hand, Arnold Taylor has secured for himself a niche in his field from which he can never be removed. And how many artists can stroll, without leaving their own home town, to a museum that, if not solely a memorial to themselves, is a monument to the comic genius that seems endemic to their birthplace and of which they have been a prominent exponent?

Some twenty years ago Derek Bamforth took me on a tour of the factory whose end-product has been endless chuckles. As he handed me card after card from their current production I wondered where were the cards I remembered from the thirties with their impossibly fat women and skinny husbands in bowlers and braces. Where were the mountains of fish and chips, the beer jars foaming like soap suds? In retrospect, those cards of the thirties seemed to snigger at miseries, whereas the sixties cards, on the whole, found life good – at least good for a laugh.

Grave and Gay

Epitaphs can be a source of humour, but I often wonder what surviving relatives thought of some of the jolly jingles carved over the last resting places of their dear departed. Some of the inscriptions may have been prepared in advance by the deceased in the manner of TV cooks, or composed by the surviving family, but surely not all. Perhaps few people could read in the days when some of the better-known comic examples were common, and thus were spared undue distress.

Not all epitaphs attempt to make light of what is in all senses a truly grave situation. There are the 'occupation epitaphs', which must have been often copied, since the same one may be encountered in a variety of places. One example is the railwayman's inscription which I first saw at Batley and which, I understand, may also be found at Newton-le-Willows in Lancashire and perhaps elsewhere:

'My engine now is cold and still,
No water does my boiler fill;
My coke affords its flame no more,
My days of usefulness are o'er.
My wheels deny their wonted speed,
No more my guiding hand they heed.
My whistle, too, has lost its tone,
Its shrill and thrilling sounds are gone.
My valves are all thrown open wide,
My flanges all refuse to glide.
My clacks, alas, though once so strong,
Refuse their aid in the busy throng.
No more I feel each urging breath,
My steam is now condensed in death.
Life's journey's o'er, each station passed,
In death I'm stopped and rest at last.
Farewell, dear friends, and cease to weep,
In Christ I'm safe; in Him I sleep.'

How I discovered that epitaph is quite a story in itself. As one of the most junior reporters on the *Batley News*, one of my tasks was to collect details of funerals from the cemetery. It was a thankless job and there were certainly no bouquets (not even a wreath) for me when I missed the only real story to come out of the cemetery for many a long day.

One night, someone – we never discovered who or why – had mysteriously opened a grave. Since graves were continually being opened to accommodate new occupants, there was nothing obviously unusual in the sight, so the fact went unrecorded in the *Batley News*. The first I knew of it was when I read the story of the opened grave in our rival sheet, the *Batley Reporter*!

Justifiably, as I believed, I pleaded ignorance, and for once, my usually explosive editor accepted my defence. But my professional pride was hurt and, at the suggestion of a sympathetic sub-editor, I tried to make amends by writing the story of the engine-driver's epitaph.

But while many an epitaph might well raise a smile, some graveyard legends are more likely to provoke a shudder, like this story told by the Rev Sabine Baring-Gould in his *Yorkshire Oddities*:

'An old woman – Molly Jakes, we will call her – died, or was thought to have died, and was buried by the parish. A few days after her funeral the vicar was talking to the sexton, when the latter said, drawing the back of his hand across his nose, "Ye thowt old Molly Jakes were dead, sur?"'

The startled cleric replied that of course the old woman was dead.

'Well, mebbe she is now', replied the sexton, who then revealed that after he'd covered the coffin he had thought he heard Molly 'movin' an' grum'lin' under t' greeand'.

'You dug her up at once, man?' the parson enquired.

'Nay', said the sexton, 't' parish paid one buryin'; who was to pay for diggin' 'er up an' putting her in ageean, if she died once maire? Besides', he added, 'old Molly cost t' parish hef-a-croon a week when she war wick (alive). Noo she's felted (hidden) under t' greeand she costs nowt. If I'd dug her up and she'd lived ever seah (so) long, what would t' ratepayers ha' said to me?'

In the church at Bolton-on-Swale near Richmond may be read a florid memorial, composed by the master of Magdalene College, Cambridge, to Henry Jenkins, reputedly Yorkshire's oldest man, who died in 1670 aged 169.

In the 1660s he was called as witness when the Vicar of Catterick was claiming an ancient right to collect tithes from parishioners. Henry was able to prove at York Assizes that to his own knowledge, tithes of wool and lambs had been paid to the vicar for at least 120 years.

One day, so the story goes, a lawyer went to see Henry, whose evidence he wanted for another case. In the garden of the cottage he saw a white-haired old man sitting in the sun. The lawyer explained his errand. 'Tha'd better ask mi fayther inside', said the old man. In the house the lawyer found an old man sitting by the fire. Neither could he help, it appeared, because his memory wasn't what it used to be. This time the suggestion was 'Ask mi fayther – he's choppin' sticks at t' back o' t' house.'

Need I tell you that the ancient chopping wood was the original Henry Jenkins? Please yourself whether you believe that one! There's certainly evidence that Henry was still swimming in the River Swale when he was past his century, with his great noble beard floating around him.

Just how Henry viewed death when at last it caught up with him, I don't know. Was he ready to 'shuffle off this mortal coil', tired perhaps of being asked silly questions or dragged off to give evidence in court cases? Perhaps, like so many other inhabitants of North Yorkshire in those days, he saw death as a journey fraught with pitfalls and traps which must be successfully negotiated if you were to arrive safely at your desired destination.

A grim poem with this theme, called the *Lyke Wake Dirge*, has given rise to the Lyke Wake Walk, a forty mile trek from Osmotherley across the moorland to Ravenscar on the coast. For more than two centuries the dirge was chanted over newly-dead corpses in North Yorkshire, as if to tell them what lay ahead and how their actions during their earthly life would aid or hinder them in their journey to the next:

'When thoo fra hither gans away,
Ivvery neet an' all,
Ti Whinney Moor thoo cumst at last,
An' Christ tak' up thi soul.
If ivver thoo gavest hosen or shoon,
Ivvery neet an' all,
Clap tha doon, an' put 'em on,

An' Christ tak' up thi soul.
But if hosen an' shoon thoo niver ga' neean,
Ivvery neet an' all,
T' whinnies [thorns] 'll prick thi sair to t' beean,
An' Christ tak' up thi soul'

Not a subject for humour, you might think, but it's the Yorkshire
way to extract humour from the most unlikely sources, which helps
to explain why Bill Cowley, founder and 'Chief Dirger' (chairman) of
the Lyke Wake Club, issued a challenge in 1955 to anyone to walk
what is now the Lyke Wake route in one day. A mixed bag of thirteen
climbers accepted his challenge and twelve out of the thirteen 'did it
in one'. Thus the Lyke Wake Club was born, and a more typically
macabre piece of Yorkshire carry-on it would be hard to find.

Not only do they have a Chief Dirger in Bill and a Chief Witch in
Jean Cowley, but the club's hierarchy includes an 'Anxious Almoner'
as well as 'Harrassed Archivists', 'Doctors of Dolefulness', 'Masters of
Misery' and 'Reluctant Report Readers'.

The Anxious Almoner himself, who described many of these dismal
doings for me, had for twenty-five years held the post of Most
Miserable and Melancholy Mace-bearer. Between 1960 and 1991,
he had made the forty mile Lyke Wake crossing from Osmotherley
to the coast at Ravenscar no fewer than thirty-five times. He also
organises the club's annual races.

There are also social events, called 'Wakes', needless to say, to
which no-one in 'ordinary clothing' is admitted. You might think that
slogging over forty miles of desolate moorland would be enough to
qualify you not only for membership of the club but to participate in
its 'evenings of mourning', 'Hallowe'en Wakes' or 'Lyke Wake
Olympics'. Not so! You must attend dressed in black, perhaps as a
mortician, a druid, an ancient Briton, a witch or a warlock, prepared
to compete for the title of 'Worst dressed Witch', 'Champion Bog-
Dodger' or whatever. The main thing is to play your part to the
utmost in ensuring that 'A Bad Time is Had by All'!

There seems to be no doubt that Yorkshire folk enjoy being
miserable, or at least pretending to be. Some of our classic jokes have
to do with funerals and death-beds. When I was a junior reporter
(with a special responsibility for funerals) I would often call at local
houses seeking details of the deceased for inclusion in an 'obit', the
potted biography which recounted whatever claims the deceased

might have had to local fame. Far from resenting what might now be seen as an 'intrusion on private grief', the surviving relatives saw it as a perfectly proper procedure: and indeed modern psychiatry emphasises the therapeutic value to the bereaved of talking about their loss.

Not surprising, therefore, that they were grateful for the local journalist's questions and very often politely invited him to view the body. It would have seemed churlish to refuse, though there were times when you didn't quite know what to say. Local neighbours seemed to be under no such difficulty. 'Ee, doesn't he (or she) look beautiful (or peaceful)?', they would exclaim in the days when shared hardships gave a value to neighbourliness such as we rarely see today, and when death had still to become cloaked in taboo. Visitors to the shrines of the newly-departed knew what was expected of them and readily offered it, greatly to the comfort of those left behind.

But even sympathy can be overdone. Striving, perhaps, for originality, one viewer of a corpse remarked: 'Ee, doesn't 'e look *well*?'

'He owt to', snapped the grieving widow. 'It's nobbut a week sin' 'e came back from 'is 'olidays at Brid!'

As a moorland doctor, R W S Bishop was often called to rural funerals, or 'sidings' as they used to be called. He discovered that Dalesmen's memories were long and that the dear departed were revered long after their passing. Hence this story of how, one day, an artist wandered into a remote dale in search of a place to work for a few months, and soon found what seemed the ideal spot, with not only good food and comfortable rooms, but a lake nearby with plentiful rushes. What a place for him to fulfil a long-cherished ambition to paint a picture on the theme 'Moses in the Bullrushes'!

He could hardly wait to get started and the work went so well that he finished the picture in good time and was so pleased with it that he decided to 'launch' it at the scene of its execution.

All the locals were invited, including the largest farmer in the dale, who was rendered almost (but not quite) speechless by the sight of the great Israelite in infancy sleeping in his floating cradle amid the bullrushes.

'So that's little Moses!', exclaimed the farmer. 'Why that beats all. 'Oo lang wad ye say he'd been dead?'

'About 3,000 years', hazarded the painter.

'Three thousand years, ye say, an' ye've painted 'im just like 'e was! Ah tell ye, ye're a varry clever fella.'

The artist looked suitably modest while a long silence ensued. It was finally broken when the farmer said, 'Ah wish ye'd come an' paint mi feyther. Ah'll pay ye for it, o' course. 'Ow much a foot do yer charge?'

It was not a question of money, the painter explained. He'd be happy to do it just to show his gratitude for the kindness everyone had shown him during his stay in the dale. 'If you'll have the old gentleman ready about two o'clock tomorrow afternoon I'll be down to make a start.'

'Have 'im ready?' echoed the farmer, 'why 'e's bin dead these forty years!'

Now it was the painter who looked astonished.

'Then how am I to paint him?'

'If ye can paint Moses who's bin dead 3,000 year, why can't yer paint mi dad who died nobbut forty year sin?'

Finding this logic unanswerable, the painter requested a photograph of the deceased. None was available, but 'He was varry like me', helpfully vouchsafed the farmer. 'Onnyroad, yer mun do t' best yer can – it'll be reight.'

No effort was spared by the painter to conjure from the past the farmhouse kitchen that was to be the setting for the portrait. He was even able to recreate the beloved old sheepdog from its skin, now serving as a rug, and doubtless wished he had something as helpful to assist him to produce a likeness of the main sitter.

When at last the work was complete, he called in the farmer and, very nervously, invited his inspection. For some time the latter appeared speechless. Then:

'Well, by gum!', he said at last. 'Ah telled thi tha wor a clever feller, but that didn't say t' orf on it. It fair knocks Moses for six, does this.'

He examined the picture in minute detail, telling the painter the name and origin of t' awd this and that, including t' awd dog Rover as if the artist had not himself studied and selected every item. 'Theer's 'is aud pipe an' 'is sup o' gin an' watter . . .' Again the farmer fell silent, for so long, this time, that the artist began to feel his qualms renewed.

The farmer's eyes were still fixed on his dead father's face when he spoke at last.

'Ah'll tell thi summat though. T' aud lad 'asn't 'arf altered!'

But Dr Bishop's main funerary recollections had to do with wills and the gargantuan funeral teas which accompanied the burial of anybody who had 'two ha'pence to rub together'.

'An old farmer was dying, and the owner of his farm, with his wife, had walked over the moor to enquire about him and if possible to see him. The old housewife, who was notoriously mean and miserly, made them a cup of tea, explaining that she was too poor to provide more than simple bread and butter for their entertainment. Unfortunately, this was overheard by a grandchild, who, childlike, exclaimed, "Ooh, grandmother, there's such a beautiful cake in the cupboard". The old woman shouted angrily, "Hod thi noise, doan't ye know t' cake's for t' burying?"'

My own favourite among such stories has been told before, but no chapter on 'sidings' would be complete without it. Old Sara Jane was generally considered to be on her deathbed. There she was lying now, downstairs in the kitchen of her cottage to make life easier for her harassed daughter, Annie, who was 'doing everything' for her, in addition to performing her own duties as mother and farmer's wife. From the fireside oven issued whiffs of roasting ham, tempting enough to tantalise the nostrils of the dead – and even of those regarded as very close to that state!

Sara Jane sniffed appreciatively, but Annie was far too busy to notice. Sara Jane sniffed louder, adding a sigh for good measure. Still no response from Annie.

'That 'am smells fair grand', persisted Sara Jane. Still silence. Then, bravely, 'Ah think Ah could fancy a bit for mi tea . . .'

And now Annie realised that action was called for before things got quite out of hand.

'Thee get on wi thi deein'', she snapped. 'Yon 'am's for t' funeral, not thee.'

Later, against all expectations, Sara Jane rallied to such a degree that she was thought well enough to be taken back upstairs. But her daughter was not going to be caught out by any flash in the pan. She handed her mother her dead father's heavy old ash plant.

'For use in emergencies,' she explained grimly. 'An' mak' sewer tha doesn't dee baht thumpin'!'

Language of Fun and Sincerity

If I hadn't caught the flu, coming home from that temperance meeting at the Ploughmans Arms, I should probably have begun this chapter differently. Something like this, perhaps:

Ah telled 'em Ah'd write a piece abaht dialect for this 'ere book, an' nah, when it cooms to dooin' it, Ah'm blowed if Ah knaw wheer to start. Ther's a reight lot o' confusion abaht dialect, tha sees. Ther's some fowk 'at think ther's nowt to it but 'ee by gooms an' sithas, an' ther's others – wod yer believe? – think it's summat to laugh at. Some fowk'd laugh if they saw a fresh-baked Yorkshire puddin' run ovver bi a tram!

And there are others whose education has been so neglected that they can't read their own native Yorkshire tongue when it's set down before them in plain black and white. So now, out of consideration for such unfortunates, I will revert to standard English for a spell, just to give them a chance to untangle their tonsils.

Ask such people if Yorkshire dialect is dying and they will probably reply: 'Yes, and the sooner it's buried, the better'. Some might say dialect was not so much dying as being tortured to death by non-Yorkshire actors in Yorkshire plays, who seem to think that a good nasal whine, a talking speed of ten words a minute and a facial expression denoting amiable lunacy are all you need to wow them in *When We are Married*.

When I was a lad, speaking 'broad Yorkshire' was the mark of a man, at least in the industrial West Riding. You talked posh at your peril. To do so was not just effete, it was an insult to your audience. They didn't talk posh and if you did, you could only have one motive, and that was to suggest that you were better than they were. Hence, a lad who had won a scholarship to the grammar school felt obliged to pronounce it 'schooil' to demonstrate his solidarity with the common people – not that they'd have accepted the description 'common' for one moment. 'Ther's nowt common abaht me', they'd have retorted if you'd been fool enough to suggest it. 'We're plain workin' fowk but we're nooan common!' And of course they were right.

Alan Bennett, who has an almost miraculous flair for putting his finger on our Yorkshire singularities, has familiarised us with his mother's characteristic use of 'common'. Anyone who knows Yorkshire knows exactly what she meant. 'Common' described something hovering somewhere between bad taste and immorality. A hairdo could be common, so could loud behaviour, adultery or a failure to rinse your milk bottles before placing them on the step. Folk who had more brass than was good for them were often common. So was a 'blawtch', the blisteringly descriptive word for a noisy, vulgar woman.

Dialect, on the other hand, was anything but common: it was the language of sincerity, into which folk lapsed (or to which they rose, perhaps) under the stress of great emotion. It was the native folk speech and it evoked affection through its associations with times past; with memories, of characters and experiences, mellowed by the passage of time.

It was also a battle cry, a declaration of unity in the face of what we regarded as a hostile world. And it often defeated its own ends by overdoing things:

'Hear all, see all, say nowt,
Sup all, eyt all, pay nowt.
An' if tha ivver does owt for nowt
Allus do it for thissen.'

That, supposedly, is the advice of a typical Yorkshireman to his son. It is thrown up at us as a reproach by every species of foreigner, but have you ever heard it offered as anything remotely resembling serious advice? Of course not. I would not attempt to explain, clever as I am, why Yorkshire folk delight in blackening their own characters – but woe betide any outsider rash enough to take them at their own evaluation. You might as well try agreeing with a woman while she's criticising her own husband!

Believe it or not, Yorkshiremen aren't the only ones who denigrate our noble breed! There are others, alas, without the excuse of our native modesty, who can't resist the temptation to have a crack at us. That classic example known as *The Yorkshireman's Coat of Arms*, for instance, can only be the product of naked jealousy.

Much perfectly good ink has been wasted on this truly 'common' insult and I don't propose to waste much more. Our coat of arms, according to this scurrilous piece of doggerel, comprises a flea, a fly, a magpie and a bacon flitch (side of a pig), and the verse begins:

'A flea will bite whoever it can,
An' soa, my lads, will a Yorkshireman.'

It goes on to point out that a fly will sup with anyone, a magpie 'can talk for a terrible span', while a flitch is 'noa gooid till it's hung'. In each case, the same characteristic is alleged to be found in the Yorkshireman.

If it's true, as some believe, that this diatribe actually originated within the county, then it can only be one more example of the Yorkshireman's disastrous capacity for self-denigration. And this arises from his failure to appreciate that outsiders don't comprehend his deadpan humour. I risk being run out of the Ridings on a rusty nail for saying it, but in my view our much-loved Yorkshire anthem is yet another example of this, and might be considered equally calamitous if we cared tuppence what those lesser breeds thought about us.

Ilkla' Moor Baht 'At is supposed to have originated as an impromptu composition by a West Riding chapel choir on a charabanc outing to Ilkley in 1805. Using the hymn-tune 'Cranbrook', they invented the tale of a young man who goes courting, hatless, on Ilkley Moor, catches a fatal chill, is buried, consumed by worms, which in turn are 'etten' by ducks. The ducks are duly 'etten' by 'us' (the choir), who are thus convicted out of our own mouths of cannibalism – a nicely gruesome, and truly Yorkshire finishing touch.

Having covered this subject in a previous book (*Yorkshire Laughter*), I'll resist the temptation to deal with it here at length. Coming, as I do, from the home of so-called 'shoddy' cloth, my instinct is never to waste good material by using it nobbut once. But I'll content myself by saying that although our famous tribal chant was never intended to be owt but a bit of 'omely fun, as Wilfred Pickles used to say, it does much to convince an uncomprehending world that we are barmy!

Why, and here I risk losing my Yorkshire passport, can't we have an anthem that in its wit, literacy and tunefulness matches what the Geordies have in *Blaydon Races*? In *Yorkshire Life* magazine I once offered a prize for the best alternative Yorkshire anthem, but although some of the entrants made a worthy showing, none of their efforts caught on, or we wouldn't still be chanting that tired old dirge about 'wurrums' and ducks.

The real trouble with dialect is that we don't quite know what to do with it, except laugh at it. But as Jack Danby, a former chairman of the Yorkshire Dialect Society and an authority on the dialect of the East Riding, told me, our Yorkshire dialects were among the regional languages once spoken all over England and are a worthy inheritance.

If you want to annoy Jack, you might try talking to him about 'the King's' or 'the Queen's' English. He will explain to you that for more than 300 years after the Norman Conquest, the so-called 'King's English' was actually French, which was the language of the court, just as Latin was the language of the Church, the schools and the universities.

I suppose (and though this is my opinion, it may not be Jack's) that as time went by, the so-called 'standard' English, which emerged from the regional languages (or dialects), became the 'official', educated or 'polite' way to communicate. Could anyone, if he'd tried, have thought up a more effective way to divide people and introduce a 'class system'?

Dialect may or may not be dying, but accents survive and are even more a target for snobbery than dialect used to be. Albert Modley, probably the best-loved of all Yorkshire comedians, once told me, 'Wear a flat 'at an' fowk think yer daft'. With equal truth he might have said, 'Speak with broad vowels and they invariably assume you're ignorant'. Nothing perplexes me more than the surprise of otherwise intelligent, 'educated' Southerners when they discover that someone can speak with a Northern accent and be at least as bright as they are.

But enough of this solemn, disputatious stuff! There's plenty of good fun in dialect, and not least in some of the delightfully descriptive names for everyday things. If there were any justice, we'd be able to slap a preservation order on words, as well as buildings. Do you know, for instance, the East Riding dialect word for earwig? Twitchbell, you say? Well, at least you're half right, because there are two: the other is forking robber, and both of them are at least as interesting as earwig.

It's easy to be sentimental about dialect, forgetting that in some present-day cases it sounds darned ugly! I think it would be astonishing if dialect, as the language of the under-privileged, had not taken on an aggressive tone, considering all that the under-privileged have been through over the years.

We talk today about 'protest songs' as if they were something new. They're not, of course. Rabbie Burns wrote them in his native Scots tongue, and Yorkshire poets, too, have used their home-spun speech to sing of the sufferings of the poor. Such a poet was Ben Preston of Bradford, born in 1819, the son of a handloom weaver. Mechanisation brought misery to the handloom weavers, who were herded into mills after what must have seemed in retrospect an almost idyllic existence, and Ben himself suffered much ill-health from working in bad conditions in the woollen warehouses of Bradford.

Here, much abbreviated for the sake of those who can take so much dialect and no more, is one of Ben's poems:

My Gronfather's Grave

Nut a puff stirred a leaf o' them grand owd trees
'At o'ershadowed the grahnd ov ahr village church,
As I gloared wi' full een on a gorse-covered heap
Under t' shade of a knotted an' time-worn birch.

Clois at hand a fine marble wor placed aboon t' squire,
Thau he stale fro' his tenants ther hard-won breead,
For it's tyrants 'at grunds us wi' pahr an' brass,
'At we honour an' worship alive or deead.

But ye'll fynd nauther tablet, nur name, nur date
Ovver t' spot wheer my gronfather sleeps i' t' dark,
For this world tak's na gaum ov a sweeatin' slave
'At can nobbut do useful an honist wark.

Fro' five ov a mornin' to nine at neet
He slaved for a livin' for forty year,
An' all t' pleasure 'at sweetened that bitter life
Wor a Sunday stretch an' a pint o' beer.

Poor grondad, I wish tha wor here to see
Hah bravely we've battled wi' pahr an' brass,
For t' day draws near when a king munnot craw
Ovver t' ignorant, impadent workin' class.

When I think o' t' long ahrs an' o' t' slavish wark
'At browt tha so sooin tuv a naamless tomb,
My courage revives, an' my arm an' neiv
Gets strung up an' doubled for t' feyt to come.

Stirring stuff, and it no doubt brought cheers from the regulars when Ben recited in the pub he kept at Gilstead after inheriting £500 and leaving the slavery of industrial Bradford. For all his hard work he lived to be over ninety, presumably a good deal more than his 'grondad' managed. I offer no glossary to explain difficult words – tha mun figure 'em aht for thissen.

Dialect need not always be defiant. Folk speech quite untainted by bitterness can hold a beauty all its own. Or perhaps it's all really a matter of who's using it.

I can never talk about dialect for long without mentioning Kit Calvert of Hawes, an archetypal Dalesman if ever there was one – farmer, cheesemaker and much else, whose battered trilby and stumpy clay pipe were a less than adequate disguise for the sensitive, subtle and highly intelligent personality they never quite managed to conceal.

I've mentioned Kit in previous books, notably one called *Yorkshire: the Dales*, a copy of which I sent him. In return he presented me with a slim, yellow-backed copy of *Wensleydale Dialect* 'by Kit Calvert, Daleman, an anthology of poetry by local folk'. Its title page, printed in a sort of 'rustic' typeface which a local printer must have had for many years, and which looked exactly suited to its purpose, bore the words: 'Chapters from the New Testament translated into the Wensleydale Tongue by Kit Calvert'. I love Kit's expression 'the Wensleydale Tongue' – no nonsense about 'dialect' – and I think Jack Danby would approve too.

Kit's New Testament translations, I am assured, are in the archives of the BBC. If so, it's a pity we don't hear them more often, because they're masterpieces, and none more so than his Wensleydale version of The *Twenty-Third Psalm*:

'The Lord is my Shipperd: Ah'll want fer nowt.
He lets m' bassock i' t' best pasture, an' taks m' bi' t'
watter side whar o's wyet an' peeaceful.
He uplifts mi soul an' maks things seea easy 'at Ah can dew
w'at's reet an' glorify His neeam.
Evan if Ah cu' t' deeath's deursteead Ah's nut bi
freetened, fer He'll be wi' me.
His creuk an' esh plant'll uphod me.
Thu puts on a good meeal afore me, reet anent them 'at
upbraids me. Thu ceuls mi heead wi' oil
an' Ah've meeat an' drink t' spar'.
Seurlie Thi goodniss an' mercy 'al bi mine fer
o' t' days o' mi life, an' Ah'll beleng t' t' hoose
o' the Lord fer ivver.'

Symptoms

I should have known better than to risk going to the doctor straight after reading dear old Dr Bishop's book about his moorland patients and their mind-boggling dialect. My problem (well, one of my problems, along with hay fever, the dog, my word processor and the family) is that I'm altogether too suggestible.

Another of my problems is my doctor. No, that's not fair. Before I get the race relations board on my tail, let me hastily point out that he's a delightful man and a first-class medico. But is he really one of us? Not unless there's such a thing as a Chinese Yorkshireman.

He has a smile like sunrise on the Yangtze, speaks perfect English, and has an uncanny knack of somehow divining the real reason for his patients' visits through a verbal smoke-screen that puts you in mind of a 1920s mill chimney. I visited him while still reeling from an overdose of Bishop's bewildering book.

I can't quite remember what was wrong with me. I know it was nothing trivial, because I only ever visit the doctor when I've discovered from our medical encyclopaedia that my life is seriously endangered. As if I hadn't enough problems already, my wife now tells me I'm a hypochondriac! Some day I must look that up – it certainly sounds painful enough to be one of mine.

'Good morning', said Dr Wu (which isn't his real name, because I can't spell that). 'What seems to be the trouble?'

Normally I would have mumbled some suitably deferential reply, because, like most folk, even in Yorkshire, I treat the medical profession with about five times the exaggerated respect shown by my caveman ancestors for the local witch doctor. So you can imagine my horror when from my own mouth another voice seemed to issue, a voice so devoid of proper reverence for anything wearing a stethoscope that I came out in a cold sweat.

'Nay', said the voice, truculent and belligerent in equal proportions, 'that's what Ah'm payin' thee to finnd aht!'

Could I really have said such a thing? How could I doubt it? There were only the two of us there, and I was sure my Chinese doctor couldn't have said those words if you'd waved a million yuan note under his nose.

How would he punish me for such irreverence? Visions of Chinese torture administered under the guise of acupuncture flashed through my mind. But Dr Wu merely smiled with the serenity of a Buddhist icon and begged pardon for his unworthiness because he didn't quite understand my supremely beautiful English. I opened my mouth to stammer an apology but all that came out was, 'Why doesn't tha ask me what me pleeans is?'

'Pleeans?', echoed Dr Wu. 'Pleeans – what, please, is pleeans?'

'Pleeans, pleeans!', I found myself repeating. 'Ax me what's up wi me! Ah's that bad Ah doan't knaw Ah to tell thi. Ah've been sweeatin' like a stuck pig ivver sin' Ah copped a perishment o' cowd last Setterda' neet comin' 'ome fra' t' Ploughmans Airms.'

'Can you tell me a little more about your symptoms,' murmured Dr Wu in a voice that would have soothed a sex-mad komodo dragon. I had never admired him more.

'Ah've nooan coom 'ere to blether abaht symptoms. Ah want nowt to do wi' sich new-fangled stuff. Ah'm despert, Ah tell thi. Tha mun cure me or it'll be all owered wi' me – Ah'll be off to t' sidin' grahnd afooar tha knaws it!'

'I see,' said Dr Wu, gently. But did he?

'Have you any pain?'

'Pain? Pain?', screeched the voice (my voice, as I now had to admit with a rising sense of horror). I vowed I'd never read another line of Bishop as long as I lived. Not that I could expect to be around much longer if I were to believe this demon with a death wish that possessed me now.

'Where exactly is the pain?', enquired Dr Wu, looking at me over his half-moon spectacles.

'Wheer is it? Wheer is it, tha says?', I screamed like a Chinese banshee (the worst kind!). 'It's ivverywheer – in mi shackles, mi belly, mi heead, mi back. They're all warkin' like hummer. Ah tell thi, man, t' pain's past bahdin'. An' if that weren't bad enough Ah'm fair ovver-run wi' t' ditherum-dotherums.'

What happened next raised my Chinese doctor even higher in my estimation. Perhaps, simply because he comes from China, with its umpteen dialects, a bit of old-fashioned broad Yorkshire, once he gets the hang of it, is summat 'e can tak' in 'is stride. (By gow, Ahm at it ageean!) But whatever the reason may be, both as a linguist and a diagnostician he leaves my medical encyclopaedia standing.

'Tha'rt gerrin' thissen all of a lather ovver nowt', said Dr Wu. 'If Ah didn't know thi better Ah'd say tha wor a bone-idle bowdykite wi' nowt on thi mind but liggin' i' bed an' 'evin' other fowk runnin' their legs off waitin' on thi. But for once, tha'rt reight – there is summat wrang wi' thi.'

'Is it fatal?', I asked with a mounting sense of dread. 'Oh, doctor, tell me the worst!'

'Flu,' said Dr Wu, as he suddenly appeared at my bedside with my wife. He handed her a prescription and turned to go. 'A bit delirious,' he said, 'but he's had a good sleep.'

'And a pretty rotten dreeam!', I shouted after him.

The Society Humorist

I'm not at all sure Major J Fairfax-Blakeborough, from whatever heavenly paddock he looks down, will forgive me for writing this chapter on a word processor. He would consider a quill pen much more appropriate and I can't help thinking he'd be right. I guess it will irritate him, too, if I call him a legend. But, cliché or not, I can't think of a better word to encapsulate a man whose life spanned so many decades and who was active in so many spheres.

Perhaps I'd better start again, because much of what I've written so far sounds too pompous and stuffy to describe 'JFB'. It could indeed be the fault of this word-processor. Maybe the spirit of one who wrote with a quill pen just will not communicate through a technological instrument undreamed of when he was born in 1883, the sort of thing against which his soul was still protesting eighty years later. Admittedly, his final copy was presented in typescript, though his machine must have been almost as old as his quill. Yet by one method or another he was always on time with his 'Sporting Notes' for *Yorkshire life*, in addition to which he managed to produce over a hundred books.

There were books about Yorkshire and books about racing, for the major came of that North Yorkshire stock ('North Riding!', he would doubtless insist) for whom a world without horses would be no world at all. An ex-cavalry officer, he was clerk of the course at a number of race venues when I first met him, though I already knew all sorts of stories about him — apocryphal or otherwise.

He was not only a legend in himself, but also a fruitful source of legends, especially horsey ones. 'Rattle a harness over a Yorkshire-man's grave and he'll wake up and steal your horse!', he would say, though I'm certain he never expected that particular old saw to be taken seriously. He was, of all men, the stoutest defender of the good name of his native county. Nothing infuriated him so much as the so-called 'Yorkshireman's coat of arms', identifying us with every kind of knavery. He must have written thousands of words denouncing it as the basest of libels.

In an article he wrote for *Yorkshire Life* in 1959 (his seventy-seventh year) entitled 'Bees from an Old Bonnet', JFB said he was the oldest of Turf officials and held the unique record of having acted as judge, clerk of the scales, starter, stake holder and club secretary, as well as in other roles. He had been called, he said, 'the most unpopular Turf official in the North' by some, resentful that they had been denied free racecourse tickets and other favours. Besides quill pens, he liked cut-throat razors, old clothes, old wine, old wood on the fire and old friends. And he hated sub-editors who, he claimed, cut out the 'best bits' in his copy. But don't we all?

He was proud to be the son of Richard Blakeborough, a Yorkshire author-playwright whom he obviously considered his superior in every way, 'a genius' at everything 'except making money', he said. Richard Blakeborough, who rejoiced (if that is really the word) in the title 'society humorist', produced a monumental Yorkshire classic (with title to match) in his *Wit, Character, Folklore and Customs of the North Riding of Yorkshire* (first published in 1898). He was, in JFB's eyes, nothing less than a paragon of innumerable virtues, and as his book reveals, he could certainly 'tell a good tale'.

Richard Blakeborough, who died in 1918, when JFB was with his cavalry regiment in France, wrote and told his stories in a North Riding dialect too broad perhaps for easy reading by the majority today, but they translate easily enough, and whether the language is Yorkshire or Icelandic, the humour is universal. Furthermore, though his stories inevitably must date, their underlying comedy is timeless, as in the tale which follows . . .

North Yorkshire was never a hotbed of socialism, certainly not a hundred years ago, so socialists were long considered fair game for a joke – like one recent convert to that creed, who, like most converts, was keen to win others to his new-found faith – this time in a system of fair shares for all. 'Nobody wi' nowt no more nor anybody else,' he explained, and all, apparently, activated by brotherly love.

'Dosta mean', asked his friend, 'that if tha'd two hosses and Ah 'edn't one, tha'd gie me one o' thine?'

'Of course Ah wod, an' Ah'll tell thi summat else, if Ah 'ed two cows an' tha 'edn't one, Ah'd gie thee one o' my cows as sooin as tha assed me for it. Tha must admit it's a grand system. Doesn't tha think tha owt to join t' socialists thissen?'

But his friend was still exploring the notion.

'Let's say tha 'ad two,pigs –' he began, 'an' Ah – '

'Ere, 'od on a bit', said the socialist, 'don't rush things too cloise – tha knaws Ah've gotten two pigs!'

The village orchestral society was rehearsing for a concert to be given the following week. The squire had dutifully dropped in, by invitation of the conductor, accompanied by his friend, who thought himself no end of an authority on music.

'Splendid noise, what?', said the squire, an affable gent, keen to support all village ventures, but no authority on matters musical.

His friend was clearly less enthusiastic.

'If only they had a horn', he said sadly.

The squire called the conductor over.

'Smithers', he said, 'we need a horn.'

'I don't know anyone as plays an 'orn', said the conductor. 'An' if we 'ad one there wouldn't be time to practise with it before t' concert.'

'But we must have one', said the squire, convinced now that the honour of the village demanded it.

Inwardly cursing the squire's knowledgeable friend, the conductor felt he must at least appear to be rising to the occasion.

'Where could we get a horn-player, an' 'ow much would it cost?', he reluctantly enquired.

'Oh, you could get one for as little as . . . five pounds', said the squire's musical friend.

'FIVE PUND?', exploded the conductor, but the squire raised a reassuring hand.

'Leave that to me, Smithers', he said. 'We need a horn and I'll see to it that we get one.'

On the night of the concert the horn player duly arrived and took his place among the other players, undeterred by the somewhat frosty reception offered to this expensive import.

The conductor raised his baton, launching the orchestra, complete with horn, into the overture to *Carmen*.

Suddenly both orchestra and audience were startled as the conductor smartly tapped his music stand and the notes tailed unmelodiously away.

'Thoo', said the conductor to the horn player, 'isn't blawin'.'

'Of course not,' that musician replied, 'this is where I take forty-five bars rest.'

'Sitha', the conductor told him, 'Ah've paid five pund for t' neet for thee, an' for five pund tha'll puff all t' way through!'

Blakeborough's title of 'society humorist' has a quaint ring today, suggestive of a kind of court jester to the nobility. A privileged role, it might seem, though some of his stories strike a sad note. Here, you might think, was a man in a kind of limbo between the gentry and the servants, not really belonging to either.

The servants, however, were in no doubt what they thought of him, especially the everlastingly outspoken coachmen. One such, apparently upset by one of Blakeborough's 'turns' at another house, complained about him to his noble employer.

'He's got impidence for owt', he declared. 'He tak's t' sarvants an' t' quality off all alike. Ah reckon nowt to 'im.'

'I'm sorry about that, said his lordship, 'because he's coming here to entertain at my son's coming of age.'

'Comin' 'ere?', demanded the horrified menial. 'Wheer will yer put 'im? T' sarvants weean't want 'im.'

'He'll dine with us, of course.'

'Wi' you? Well, yer mun excuse me, mi lord, but Ah reckon yer goin' to mak' a reight common do on it!'

Having once spent three days at a house party in his capacity as society humorist, Blakeborough was told by the coachman who took him to the station that if that was all he did for a living, he got it easy!

'Yer fed for nowt, yer expenses are paid, yer travel for nowt, yer sheltered for nowt an' yer do nowt. Yer nowt but an aristocratic pauper!'

But didn't brains come into the matter, asked Blakeborough.

'Brains? BRAINS?', exploded the coachman. 'Ah've as many brains as thee if they were all scraped oot!'

Leeds Lad Made London Laugh

Phil May was artist, drunk, joker and saint all rolled into one. One night when he was disturbed by a burglar, he persuaded the man to talk as a friend and drink whisky with him through the night. Another night, hoping to placate his wife when he was late home, he took her a five foot conger eel. Once he found a tramp sleeping on a bench in the winter cold, covered him with his expensive new fur coat and walked home through the snow in his jacket.

Leeds-born May was a tragi-comic genius who revolutionised the art of the cartoon and died of drink at an early age. His drawings, famous a hundred years ago, were published in dozens of leading periodicals and in his 'Annuals', which appeared without a break from 1892 to 1903. But although May himself has been justly described as a 'fellow of infinite jest', some of his cartoons fail to raise a spontaneous smile today.

Their artistry cannot be denied, but in addition to their quality as works of art, demonstrated in their wonderful economy of line, they provide some of the most effective illustrations of the hypocrisy of the late Victorian/early Edwardian age, when the 'lower orders' were seen as fair game for laughter, but hardly human.

We may think ours is a cruel age, but some of May's captions were too insensitive, by our standards, easily to achieve print today. An urchin runs into a shop to ask the proprietor if he wants an errand boy. 'No', replies the shopkeeper. 'Yer do now', says the boy. 'Yours has just been runned over.'

May's 'Guttersnipes', as he labelled them, are almost invariably cheerful, self-possessed and unabashed by the toffs they encounter surprisingly often. A top-hatted, monocled gent is invited by a small drab to hold the baby she is carrying 'while I blow my nose'. Costers – the girls glorious in feather-decked hats – are shown revelling on Bank Holiday Monday. The females are usually called Arriet, the males 'Arry. Drunks and slatterns abound in May's drawings, though the drunks are taken from all classes and the toffs certainly come off worse in their encounters with the scruffs. Standing behind a top table full of unprepossessing intellectuals, one waiter observes to his colleague: 'Well, they may 'ave the intellec', Fred, but we certainly 'as the good looks!' And May's drawing in no way belies the claim.

There's little doubt whose side May is on in those graphic reports from the front line of the class war, but there are times when the jokes seem to pander to the well-off in their determination to see the *hoi polloi* as comic but contemptible. At other times they appear to provide an outlet for the uneasy conscience of the upper classes, who may have been anxious to reassure themselves with the thought that 'The poor are dirty and squalid and uneducated; they drink too much and beat their wives, but they're quite harmless really. They have a wonderful time despite their poverty and you really can't help laughing at them!'

Phil May: *Begging, The Lady and the Tramp.*

If May had lived in an earlier age he might have collaborated with Dickens, though the mood of Dickens's humour is quite different from May's. Sam Weller, for instance, is funny because he is Sam Weller, not because he belongs to the servant class. Dickens attacked the evils of his age openly, but that attitude seems rarely to be shared by Phil May. However, in his drawing *An East End Gin Shop* there seems absolutely 'nowt to laugh at'. The faces, both of the customers and the proprieter, appear brutalised and hopeless, and a slatternly mother allows her little girl to drink from her jug while her young son eagerly waits his turn. Similarly, in *East End Loafers*, a study of three men outside a gin shop, the keynote is despair unrelieved by any attempt at humour. Comparing them with some of May's supposedly comic down-and-outs it is easy to believe that, in these drawings, Phil May is not merely exercising his artistry but illustrating a tragedy that he shared.

After his death a collection of sketches was found under his bed, one of which showed Death beckoning him to join a dance of skeletons. Just a few days earlier he had written this supposedly light-hearted epitaph:

'Here lies poor old Phil
While he lived he lied his fill,
And, now he's dead,
He's lying still.'

Born in New Wortley, a suburb of Leeds, on the 22nd April 1864, Philip William May was the seventh child of Philip and Sarah Jane May, a talented but ill-starred couple. Phil's father died when he was only fifty though his mother outlived her son to die at the age of eighty-four in 1912.

Due to the family's straitened circumstances, Phil, who was only nine when his father died, started work before he was thirteen. His first job was in a solicitor's office; his next, briefly, in an estate agency, where he spilt ink on a plan. He probably saw it as a sad waste of ink and was no doubt glad to move on. Mixing paints for a scene painter at the Grand Theatre, Leeds, was much more in his line and incidentally opened up the way to his true vocation. Now he had the opportunity to draw portraits of the performers, which he sold to them at a shilling a time. He later increased his fee to five shillings and had the thrill of seeing his paintings, some of them three feet high, exhibited in frames outside the theatre. When Phil and the scene painter's son composed and acted in plays of their own, young May was the natural choice to play comic roles. Soon he was contributing drawings to local papers such as the *Yorkshire Gossip* and the *Busy Bee*.

Stage-struck, apparently from birth, he made his professional theatrical debut at the Spa Theatre, Scarborough. Here and in Leeds he played a variety of roles, continuing with his drawings and also designing pantomime costumes. But his sights were set on London. He visited an uncle in the capital who had theatrical connections, but who, after showing Phil the sights, bought the lad a ticket for Leeds and waved him off on the homeward journey – or so he thought. Phil, who had already appeared in panto as Dick Whittington's cat, got off the train as soon as possible, 'turned again' and walked back to London.

Years of struggle followed. He slept on the Thames Embankment or under carts in Covent Garden, but gradually his fortunes improved. At last he achieved publication in a London paper, the *St Stephen's Review*. Time and again, when the future looked hopeless, a benefactor, influenced perhaps by the smiling, modest young man's charm, would come to his aid. Foremost among these was his wife, Lillian, whom he met at the confectioner's shop she kept opposite the Grand Theatre in Briggate, Leeds. Lillian sold her shop and she and Phil first set up home in rooms in Bedford Street, Covent Garden.

Phil May's future career included a period in Australia, followed by a sojourn in Paris where he revelled in sketching characters he found in the boulevards and cafés. Books of his drawings and the ever-widening circle of newspapers and magazines that published his work contributed to his increasing fame and fortune. He became as much a household name as Dan Leno and according to any superficial judgement should have been a happy man.

He had wit and charm, a sunny personality and perfect manners. Yet his popularity proved a treacherous ally for it encouraged him to indulge the weakness for drink, which, together with overwork, led to his early death of phthisis (tuberculosis) and cirrhosis of the liver on the 5th August 1903 at 5 Melina Place, St Johns Wood, London. Having been recently converted to the Roman Catholic faith through the efforts of a friend, he was buried in St Marys Roman Catholic Cemetery at Kensal Rise.

Phil May died under no illusions as to the reason for his life's tragic brevity. When the portraitist J J Shannon painted him in oils, it was certainly a case of 'warts and all', despite Shannon's great admiration for his subject. May's youthful, almost elfin good looks, with piercing eyes and the fringe caused, he said, by his mother's habit of stroking his head, were little changed, but his countenance bore the unmistakable marks of alcoholism. A young girl student who met him in a Regent Street tavern was so obviously mesmerised by his nose

Phil May, a self-portrait.

that May told her it was his most expensive possession – 'it has cost me over £30,000 to acquire it'. To his portraitist Shannon, who had recently painted Sir Thomas Dewar of whisky fame, May said the two pictures should hang side by side, with the caption 'Cause and Effect'.

Phil May's facial disfigurement caused by drink must have been one of the heaviest crosses he had to bear. He was not a vain man – he had too great a sense of humour for that – but he was certainly one of the most sociable. His sensitivity about his appearance caused him to shun company, though company never shunned him. Whenever word got out that he was at any kind of gathering – hiding his light in a corner perhaps, or in some quiet room – the guests would flock to be near him.

During the unhappy later years his wife Lillian must have been his greatest comfort and he was often conscience-stricken about his treatment of her during his lapses.

Once, being brought home about 4 am from the Savage Club by a friend appointed his custodian by Lillian, he stopped in Covent Garden, then at its busiest, and had the cab filled with red roses, her favourite flowers. She woke in the morning to find herself surrounded with roses, and Phil sleeping on the sofa. On another occasion, having been despatched home in a hansom somewhat earlier, he found the market deserted, so directed the cabbie to a fishmonger's shop, roused the long-suffering proprietor and demanded a lobster. In vain the man protested from an upper window that he was completely sold out.

'Mus' have something for the missus', insisted May.

No doubt grumbling under his breath in purest Billingsgate, the fishmonger descended the stairs, flung open the door and invited May to see for himself. He saw! In a corner of the shop he found a five foot conger eel.

'This'll do!', said May.

Doubtless glad to be rid of him, the shopkeeper provided wrapping paper and May struggled to the cab bearing his dead but highly mobile peace offering, which refused to be confined by its inadequate wrapping and slithered tirelessly about the cab until May arrived home at Melina Place.

Lil not only withstood the shock of receiving such a gift but managed to find among the shiny and tattered wrapping paper some drawings May should have delivered to the office of *the Graphic*.

May had often to be taken home in his later years, but there had been many times when he had earlier performed that service for others. The story is told that John L Sullivan, the boxer, was so terrified of his wife that he persuaded May to take him home and pushed the fragile artist through his door ahead of him to be the first target for Mrs Sullivan's wrath. Doubtless May filled the role with his usual equanimity. He was not easily scared.

May's goodwill to all he met was legendary. Having bought a fine fur-lined coat with £50 from the sale of a drawing, he showed it off with pride at the Savage Club. Later that night, unable to find a cab, he set off to walk home through the bitter snowy night. On the way he found a tramp shivering in his sleep on a park bench. May knew what it was like to sleep in the park. He covered the vagrant with his new coat and went on his way.

Later, a policeman questioned the tramp about his expensive coat, which was traced to May through letters found in the pockets. To his great embarrassment the king of cartoonists had to go to court and clear the tramp's name by revealing his own generosity.

Uncle Ephraim and Superstition

'Superstitious? Me?', said Uncle Ephraim. 'Nay, I nivver am!'

'Then why did yer walk round that ladder on Mafeking Street yesterday? Cos yer were freetened o' walkin' under it, that's why. Stands to reason – yer must 'ave been.'

Alarmed by my own cockiness, I secretly measured the distance between Uncle Ephraim and me. That included what I thought of as 'the throwing distance', as well as the length of his strong right arm, for Uncle Ephraim was adept at snatching up a bit of grit from his hen-run floor and scoring a stinging direct hit on the back of my neck.

He never moved, merely continued to gaze at an obviously 'egg-bund' khaki campbell, on which he was clearly contemplating an act of euthanasia.

'One o' these days,' he said at last, 'tha'll go too far.'

Tempted by his inactivity, I still pushed my luck.

'I 'xpect tha'll say there were a fella on t' ladder wi' a pot o' paint, an' tha were freetened it ud drop on thi 'ead. Not 'at it could do much 'arm if it did . . .'

'Aw?', enquired Uncle Ephraim mildly, ''Ow does tha mek that aht?'

It was his unaccustomed mildness that undermined my confidence. I had known Uncle Ephraim long enough to be able to recognise the calm that is said to precede a storm.

'Nay, nowt', I mumbled, pacifically.

'Well if it's nowt', he observed judicially, 'why does tha keep goin' on abaht it?'

'Ah nobbut said – '

'Tha nobbut said Ah wor superstitious.'

'Well, if yer not, why did yer get so worked up t'other day when that little brown 'en crowed like a cock? Onnyroad, wheer is that little brown 'en?'

He ignored the question, merely recited:

'A whistlin' woman an' a crawin' 'en
Is nawther use to God nor men.'

'Tha's killed it!', I accused him, almost in tears. That little brown hen, no matter how confused it had been about its sexuality, had been a special friend of mine.

'Nay, there's nowt 'appened to it, except Ah've swapped it for that white bantam ovver theer.'

Now it was my turn to be confused – and not for the first time – by adult morality. If a crowing hen meant bad luck, why give the bad luck to somebody else? Anyway, Uncle Ephraim should have given his crowing hen to me – I wouldn't have minded if it had trumpeted like a bull elephant.

'Ah don't see – '

Uncle Ephraim anticipated my objections.

'Ah knaw tha doesn't. There are more things in Heaven and earth, Horatio', he quoted solemnly, 'than are dreamed of in thy philosophy. That's Shakespeare.'

'Who's he?', I sulked. 'Some'dy else yer went to schooil with? An' what were 'e on abaht when he said it?'

'He were sayin' 'at brussen little beggars like thee doan't knaw ivverything.'

'I know that, Uncle Ephraim', I assured him meekly, whilst secretly plotting revenge. 'That's why I ask thee questions . . . Cos o' thi wide experience o' life', I added pompously.

Mollified, if still suspicious, he showed his gap teeth in a grin for the first time that morning. 'What does tha want to knaw, lad?', he beamed. 'Ask me owt tha likes.'

'Why did yer get so 'et up when Ah put that pair o' booits Ah'd browt from t' cobbler's on your table?'

'Cos it's – '

'Ah knaw, bad luck. An' why did yer play Owd 'Arry when mi auntie came in t' 'ouse with 'er umbrella oppen – '

'Er – well, tha sees – '

'An' why did yer get all miserable an' start writin' yer will, t'other day when yer brok' yer shavin' mirror?'

'Sitha! Ah'll – '

'An' then yer looked rahnd for two other things to break, because these things allus come in threes, yer said, an' yer wanted to mek sure nowt else yer brok' that day would be worth owt? An' why does tha nivver tread on a blackclock, cos – '

'It's noan a blackclock, yer daft 'awporth', he roared, stung at last out of his good humour. 'It's a rainclock, an' tha 'asn't to tread on it in case it rains. Blackclocks live in cellars an' kitchens, not aht on t' road like rainclocks. Ah'm answerin' no more o' thi daft questions, yer cheeky little mork. Ah'll tell thi nowt no more. Ger off 'ome – Ah've 'ad enough o' thee today!'

'Just one more question. Go on', I wheedled.

'Well, what is it?'

'Why do yer say you're not superstitious?'

He snatched up his yard brush and threw it at me. I dodged and it hit the wall, breaking off its head.

'Nah tha's done it!', lamented Uncle Ephraim. 'Yer should nivver damage a brush in case a witch 'as ridden on it an' she cooms to get 'er awn back on yer.'

'Uncle Ephraim – '

'WHAT NOW?'

'Do you know any witches?'

You know what happens to people who ask daft questions . . .

'Goathland were t' place for witches', said Uncle Ephraim. 'That's a little place on t' moors inland fra' Whitby. Tha can get there on t' North Yorkshire Moors Railway. It's a grand little spot, but it used to be fair wick wi' witches. It did that, though t' one I knew would 'ave been more nor enough for onybody!'

He fell silent, awaiting further encouragement.

'What did they call her?'

'Which one?'

'T' one you knew.'

'What makes you think I knew only one?' (He could be touchy, my Uncle Ephraim.)

'*Tha* did! Tha said, "T' one I knew – "'

'Ah said, "T' one I knew *in Goathland*". Tha wants to wesh thi lugs aht!'

'Pardon me for breathin!', I said with devastating but wasted sarcasm. 'Well, what did they call her?'

'Nanny Pierson. Mind yer, there were two Nanny Piersons. Some fowk say there were three.'

'Gerraway – why?'

'Well, they called all grandmothers Nanny in them days, an' so any old woman were called . . . Shurrup an' let me get on wi' mi tale!'

'That's a funny name! All reight, don't get yer wig off', I said, looking fixedly at his unruly thatch.

With an air of offended dignity he produced a threadbare army beret from his pocket and placed it carefully on his head, muttering absent-mindedly about 'cheeky little morks'.

'Folk in Goathland were freetened aht o' their wits o' Nanny Pierson, but that didn't stop 'em seekin' 'er 'elp when it suited 'em . . . like t' owd squire. His dowter wanted to marry a young farmin' chap, but squire 'ad other ideas for 'er. Ther' were an owd fella with a lot more brass than good looks after 'er. Ah suppose t' squire were a bit 'ard up, like, an' thowt 'e might be able to borrow a bob or two if t' owd chap became his son-in-law.

'But as tha'll finnd aht for thissen, lasses 'as minds o' their own, though t' way they carry on sometimes makes mi wonder if "mind" is the right word!

'Onnyroad up, t' ugly owd chap got it into 'is 'ead 'at t' young woman might run off wi' her sweetheart an' so he goes to see Nanny Pierson. T' next thing we knaw, squire's dowter can't move awther of 'er legs, so there were no chance of 'er elopin' wi' onnybody.

'But that young feller 'ad a trick or two of 'is own. 'E went to see a chap they called the Scarborough Wise Man – a sort o' witch-chap – and asked 'im what 'e could do to put things reight.

'T' wise man set t' young chap in a darkened room an' browt out a lookin' glass.

'"Look in 'ere", 'e says, "an' tell me whose face tha sees."

'T' young man did as 'e were bid.

'"By gow!", 'e says, starin' into t' mirror, "that's Nanny Pierson, clear as day."

'"Ah thowt as much", said the wise man. "Nah, Ah'll tell thi what tha mun do."'

And this, as near as Uncle Ephraim could remember, was the wise man's advice to the lovelorn young farmer: somehow or other he must obtain a drop of Nanny Pierson's blood, then go to church and steal some holy water and mix that and the blood in a cup of milk from a red cow.

'Then coom t' really 'ard bit: 'e had to get into t' lass's bedroom an' rub the mixture into her calves an' t' soles on 'er feet.'

Uncle Ephraim almost brought tears to my eyes describing how the farmer's heart sank in despair. How, first of all, was the poor love-lorn lad to get a drop of Nanny Pierson's blood? If, indeed, the wizened crone's veins contained any! But he need not have despaired: in North Yorkshire villages there were few secrets and he soon found an old woman who knew all there was to know about Nanny Pearson.

This old dame told him that in a certain field every night a hare was to be seen sitting, a hare which, so far, neither dog could catch nor man snare, but if the farmer could shoot it, all his troubles might soon be over. However, since this was no ordinary hare but Nanny herself in another form, he would need a special bullet made of silver.

The young farmer was by no means rich, but his love for his darling meant more to him than the few silver coins he had to melt to make the special bullet. After that he lay in wait for a night or two on the

edge of the field where the elusive hare liked to sit. A good marksman, he hit her with his silver bullet at the first attempt. She was only wounded and scampered away like the wind, but on the grass where she had sat he found what he needed – a few drops of her blood.

"E were fair suited as tha can imagine', said Uncle Ephraim. "E still 'ad to get inside t' lass's bedroom, but that were easy after what 'e'd 'ad to do before.'

At dead of night the young farmer, carrying a bottle containing the holy water, the milk from a red cow and – most valuable of all – blood from the hare that was Nanny Pierson's secret other self, climbed a ladder to his sweetheart's window. Gently he stifled her cry of surprise and applied his magical remedy. Immediately, she was able to stand! Then, having descended the ladder with perfect ease, she went with her lover to a place of safety, and there she stayed until they were married.

'An' what 'appened to Nanny Pierson?'

'Ah doan't knaw.'

'Did she dee?'

'Ah doan't knaw, Ah tell thi.'

"Appen, when she'd been shot, she couldn't change back into an owd woman, an' she 'ad to carry on wi' bein' an 'are.'

"Ow many times do I 'ave to tell thi – AH DOAN'T KNAW!'

'Tha were theer, why dun' tha knaw? Ah think tha must 'ave made it all up.'

'Tha con think what tha likes. But Ah knaw one thing – '

'An' so do I.'

'What's that, then?', demanded Uncle Ephraim, fiercely.

'Tha'll tell mi nowt no more!'

The pot egg he flung at me only just missed its target.

How To Get Rich Quick

Patrick Ryan, in his book *How I Became a Yorkshireman*, made some penetrating observations about the residents of his adopted county. Yorkshiremen, he had noticed, never tired of singing the praises of their ancestral home and telling visiting foreigners from Lancashire or Surbiton where to go and what to see. But ask them if they themselves had seen Fountains Abbey or Rievaulx, Penyghent or the Cow and Calf Rocks, Bempton Cliffs or York Minster, and you found (or at least Patrick did) that somehow or other they've never had the time to visit these time-honoured sites.

Mind you, Patrick was a refugee from Cockneyland, so it's just possible that the Tykes he met regarded him as a southern secret agent and considered it nowt less than their patriotic duty to pull the wool (preferably from a Swaledale tup) over his curious eyes.

But there's certainly summat in what he says. Since you are reading this book you are obviously a person of some discernment, able to answer any question about Yorkshire that an inquisitive visitor from the Old Kent Road might throw at you. Or are you? Did you know, for instance, where in Yorkshire King Arthur sleeps with the knights of his Round Table, waiting for the moment when England has need of him and someone blows his horn to bring him galloping hell-for-leather to the rescue?

All right, so you're one of the clever ones who know that I'm talking about Richmond Castle. But what else do you know? Did you, for instance, know about Potter Thompson, the Richmond man who might have become the possessor of King Arthur's treasure if he hadn't lost his nerve?

It happened this way. Potter Thompson was wandering one day about his native Richmond and dreaming about King Arthur when he came upon something he'd never noticed before, the entrance to a tunnel in the castle courtyard. He had the strange sensation that something was drawing him towards the tunnel and, once he was inside, his legs seemed to be moving faster and faster of their own accord, deeper and deeper into its hidden depths.

'Hey, 'od on a minute', said Potter Thompson, 'Ah 'even't time to go pot'olin', Ah've some pots o' mi own to mek.'

He might just as well have kept his mouth shut, because all that happened was that his legs seemed to go faster still.

After a bit he came to a chamber at the end of the tunnel, and there, snoring like billyo, were a lot of chaps in armour, one of them wearing a crown on his head. It was a good job Potter Thompson wasn't carrying a tray of pots fresh from his kiln or he'd have found himself with his work to do over again.

Potter Thompson knew the crowned head belonged to King Arthur, because there, beside him, was his sword Excalibur, his great treasure chest and his horn. The potter had never seen anything so magnificent in his life. The sword particularly fascinated him. He felt sure that if he could take it away with him and sell it to some rich nobleman he would never need to throw another pot as long as he lived – except at his wife, to keep her in order.

His hand was almost on the hilt of the magnificent sword when King Arthur gave an enormous snore and stirred in his sleep. Terrified, Potter Thompson snatched back his hand, turned his back on sword, treasure and all, and ran back the way he had come as if all the fiends in hell were chasing him.

And as he ran, a ghostly voice echoed after him:

'Potter, Potter Thompson,
If thou hadst only grasped the sword or blown the horn,
Thoud'st been the luckiest man that ever yet was born.'

Next time you go to Richmond you might have a go at finding the tunnel yourself, but if you do, make sure you keep your head. Or else just carry on doing the pools – it's gentler on the nerves.

SEMERWATTER

A legend retold

Where Semerwatter's lake now lies
Amid yon' circlin' hills,
A lofty town once climbed to t' skies,
A place o' pomp an' frills.
Its fowk were rich, but shallow, too,
'Ard-hearted as their gold!
No thowts 'ad they for t' poorer fowk –
Or so the story's told.

I' Semerdale the corn grew tall,
The sheep wor fat an' sweet.
Rich fowk gate richer, wealth wor all;
Others 'ad nowt to eat!
Owd John an' 'is wife Mary Ann
Wor poor enough, by gum,
But thankful they'd a crust to spare,
Should some poor stranger coom.

John an' 'is wife lived on an 'ill,
Wi' t' town spread out beneeath.
'We've a rare view, but still',
Puffed John, 'that climb taks all mi breeath'.
'Ne'er mind, owd lad', said Mary Ann,
'It's climbin' keeps us spry,
An' livin' at this 'eight we're able
Strangers to espy'.

'There's one approachin' now', said John,
As by the door he stood,
'A beggar chap, he looks awf deead,
'Is feet are streeaked wi' blood.'
''E looks fair clemmed', said Mary Ann.

'Let's 'elp 'im on 'is way.'
'We've 'ardly owt to eyt ussens',
Said John – ''E'll 'ev to pay!'

'For shame, for shame', said Mary Ann.
'Tha caps me, John, an' reight!
Tha'd see a starvin' fella man
An' charge 'im for 'is meyt?'
'Tha's reight', said John, 'is face brick-red,
''Ere is a man i' trouble.
We'll charge 'im nowt this once – but think on,
Next time 'e pays double!'.

John 'elped the stranger to a seat
An' warmed 'im by the fire.
He stirred the embers of the peat,
And as the sparks flew higher,
'Is wife found oatcake an' some milk
An' filled a cup to t' brim;
Then washed the poor man's bloodstained feet
An' bandaged 'em for 'im.

And as the stranger's strength returned,
'E told what 'ad befell:
'Ow, beggin', 'e'd been rudely spurned,
An' told to go to 'ell!
'Only at your poor house', he said,
'Was kindness offered me –
But those rich folk who live below
Shall suffer, as you'll see!'

He stood once more within the door
And raised his hands on high.
'Rich folks', he cried, 'who spurn the poor,
Only deserve to die!'
The thunder rolled, the sky grew black,
The rain began to pour.
And as the pair in terror watched,
It filled the valley floor!

It covered every house and barn,
Each market, mill and steeple.
It drowned what once had been a town
And slaughtered all the people.
The couple closed their eyes in fear
'Gainst such a dreadful sight.
And when they opened them at last,
No stranger was in sight!

'Oh, John, I niver felt such fear,
But now the sun shines high',
Said Mary Ann. 'He who came here
Has gone, with no goodbye.
A saint he was, for sure', she mused,
'So grateful an' so civil!'
Said John: 'If that's what saints can do,
Lord save us from a divil!'

Battle of the Sexes

I had it in mind to write a chapter about the greatest Yorkshireman, until I tried to discover who he was. Apart from such obvious candidates as my Uncle Ephraim, Freddie Trueman, Arthur Scargill and our milkman, there is a pretty wide field to choose from. Then there is the difficulty of deciding on the criteria to be observed in such a contest.

Norrie Ward in his book *Yorkshire's Mine* (a pretty controversial title if ever I saw one, but then he came from Morley) had a similar problem when trying to determine our greatest and best. Ought age to come into it, he wondered. If so, Henry Jenkins, of Bolton-on-Swale, who apparently clocked up 169 years, would surely be a contender, whereas if it came to size or weight, Harry Cooper of Scugdale, at eight foot six and weighing twenty-nine stones, or William Bradley of Market Weighton (seven foot nine inches and twenty-seven stones), must be considered.

But perhaps the biggest difficulty of all, and one hardly faced in the past by authors like Norrie and me, is that according to the feminist lobby, the greatest Yorkshireman of all would have to be a woman!

Until now, the concept of female superiority was taken for granted by women everywhere: it was just too obvious to be worth arguing about. For thousands of years, women in Yorkshire and most of the civilised world, as well as Lancashire, have had not the slightest doubt that the sole reason for man's existence on earth was to provide women with, at best, a meal ticket and, at worst, amusement. But at one time women had the sense to keep quiet about it! They just carried on in their own sweet way, remembering that the hand that rocks the cradle doles out the bacca brass, and firmly believing that most men should never have got out of their cradles in the first place.

So why did women waste their time on us? They could have gone in for pigeon-racing, training circus elephants or breeding Siamese cats – and some of them did – but these creatures, while more intelligent and usually prettier than men, were (and this is the crux of the matter) less easy than men to control.

Why, you ask, should this be so? (Though if you're a woman you already know the answer and if you're a man you've never even thought of the question.) It is so, my friends, because of all the creatures on the face of the earth, man is the vainest and therefore the most vulnerable to flattery, cajolery and all the other bewitching arts practised down the ages since Eve herself was nobbut a lass.

Should you question my qualifications in this field of learning, I need only remind you that I am a former president of the Henpecked Club (described elsewhere in this volume), an organisation with which my mother-in-law could never see eye to eye and whose jokes never came near to making her laugh. She saw our brotherhood only as evidence of the criminal insanity of the male sex in general and her son-in-law in particular.

Patrick Ryan, already mentioned with due reverence in these pages, overcame the disadvantages of being a Londoner of Irish descent sufficiently to write a book called *How I Became a Yorkshireman*. It is a work towards which I feel some of the affection of a godfather, if not a midwife, since it consists substantially of articles Patrick had contributed to *Yorkshire Life* at my request when I was editor.

Fresh from the south, he appeared doubtful at first of his qualifications for the job when I mooted it over lunch at the Prospect Hotel in Harrogate.

'No need to be bashful, lad', I said. 'But thi modesty does thi credit.'

I had the impression my words of bluff commendation only unnerved him, and therefore did all I could to reassure him that in due course he would overcome his natural disadvantages and learn to talk English reight weel, 'appen even as good as what I could meself.

Patrick's book was nothing if not comprehensive, a do-it-yourself course in learning how to be a Tyke among Tykes, by one who had done-it-himself! I heartily recommend it to all immigrants to God's Own County. There are chapters on how to be a neighbour and how to cover the head (with notes on the absolute indispensability and innumerable uses of that Yorkshireman's helmet, the flat cap). Patrick's chapter on learning the language might have been considered rather presumptuous after a mere six months in the county, while Rhodes only knows how he got away with a chapter on learning about cricket – in a county that's proud to declare, 'We don't laike cricket for fun 'ere, tha knaws!'

Perhaps he was on safer ground with instruction on how to be owned by a Yorkshire Terrier, or how to be a sportsman, or even learning about t' League, which I need hardly point out was nothing at all to do with the League of Nations, the League Against Cruel Sports (like cockney baiting), or even the Primrose League.

But the moment finally came when I could say to him, with tears in my eyes, 'By gum, lad, Ah think tha's cracked it. Tha's proved thissen one of us!' It was when I had read his chapter on how to 'treat women', which had nothing, let me tell you, to do with buying them port and lemon! If anything could be said to have converted Patrick to our Yorkshire values it was the Tykes' determination to keep women in their place. And what was their chief weapon in this battle for freedom? What else but Yorkshire pudding?

According to Ryan's researches, it was the amount of indefatigable, strong-right-arm batter-beating insisted on by every right-thinking Yorkist husband (and no nonsense about electric mixers) that made the Yorkshireman master in his own home. By thus ensuring that his wife was in a permanently dizzy state he rendered her completely manageable.

But, Ryan revealed, there was much more than even Yorkshire pudding to keeping the Yorkshireman's trousers where they belonged. Some of his revelations delved not only into the realm of the esoteric but even into the Yorkshireman's garden and what he grew there – or didn't!

It was, apparently, all a matter of mint. When Patrick asked his Yorkshire employer, Mr Micklethwaite, for a few sprigs of mint to grow in his garden, that flat-cap-wearing, umbrella-scorning worthy reeled, blenched and manifested all the other classic symptoms of shock-horror. Having recovered, he explained to his protégé from the south that every Yorkshireman knew that 'mint in t' garden meant woman's work in t' 'ouse', and as long as there was breath in his body his own garden would be innocent of this pernicious weed.

This was a new one on me, but not, apparently, on Patrick's new neighbours in Leeds. After he had recklessly introduced a few sprigs of the deadly stuff into his garden (having smuggled them at great personal risk from the south), he soon noticed the pointed way in which on both sides they defended their male pride by watering their fences liberally with weedkiller.

As I say, I had never heard of the dangers of mint-growing. I have, in my happy ignorance, cultivated mint from my earliest youth. It's probably far too late to save me from the consequences now, but the least I can do is warn the younger members of the Henpecked Club, while there's still time . . .

A Fair Deal for Dragons

Yorkshire has had at least its fair share of dragons.

Take the dragon of Wantley, South Yorkshire. allegedly slain by More of More Hall. This fearsome beast – the dragon, that is – had two wings, a sting in his tail 'as long as a flail', plus forty-four iron teeth and the regulation-pattern smoking nose.

He followed what might be called a varied diet including cattle, trees, houses, churches and, sad to say, children – even well-behaved ones. In fact, it was after he had devoured three such morsels that a deputation from the kids' home village called on More (a 'furious knight' who sounds almost as much a menace as the dragon himself) to enlist his aid. His exploits included grabbing a horse by the mane and swinging him till he was dead – after which, it is recorded, he 'ate him all up but his head'.

Sighing and sobbing, the villagers beseeched More to slay this dragon. As a reward, promised the villagers, they'd give him all their goods.

They could keep their goods, said More. All he wanted was a smiling, brisk young maid of sixteen 'to anoint me o'ernight e'er I go to fight, and to dress me in the morning'. (Well, that was what he said.)

He went to Sheffield for some new armour covered in six inch spikes, which made him look like a chromium-plated porcupine. After six pots of ale 'and a quart of aqua-vitae', he felt ready for the fray. First of all, he crept into a well where he knew the dragon would come to drink, and when the dragon did so, More socked him in the mouth.

For two days and a night they battled, until the knight 'hit him a kick on the arse' (his weak spot apparently), whereupon the dragon made a somewhat melodramatic speech and died. A bit of an anticlimax, if you ask me, though we mustn't forget the knight's purpose-made armour, which presumably included spiked toe-caps.

You meet a better class of dragon-slayer at Nunnington, North Yorkshire, or at least a better story, because in this case star billing is shared between the knightly hero, one Peter Loschy, and his dog. When called upon to destroy the terrible dragon of Loschy Wood, Peter, like More of More Hall, had a special suit of armour made, but in his case reinforced with razor blades, not spikes.

As Peter, with the aid of these appurtenances, reduced the dragon to manageable portions, his dog carried away each bit to Nunnington churchyard to prevent the dragon magically reassembling itself. All seemed to be going well for the dragon-killing duo, but cheer ye not yet, because this is a dragon story with an unhappy ending – and not just for the dragon!

After a long, hard fight, Peter finally severed the dragon's head, thus apparently ensuring victory. Tail held high, his dog proudly carried the head away to join the rest, then returned to Peter to lick his face in triumph. Alas, the dog's tongue was now impregnated with the dragon's deadly venom and both dog and knight instantly fell dead.

If you doubt my word go to Nunnington, where you will see for yourself in the church the effigy of Peter and his dog, placed there by grateful villagers to honour their noble benefactor. Or will you? In fact, the recumbent stone knight in full armour really commemorates Sir Walter Teyes, a lord of the manor who died in 1325, while the 'dog' at his feet is supposed to be a lion.

Some of these knightly lions must have been mightily put out to be taken for dogs, but it happened all the time, partly because very few people living in England had ever seen a lion; and that, of course, included the masons carving the effigies. (They may also have been influenced by the amount of stone they would have needed to carve a life-size lion: even their dragons were usually on the small side.)

Clearly, in the days before people had TV screens to glue their eyes on, they gave their close attention to the things around them and did their best to account in their own terms for anything outside their experience. Very often they got it wrong, but in the process created a much better story than was warranted by the facts.

Jacqueline Simpson, in her book *British Dragons*, cites an example of such misinterpretation. On a worn gravestone at Kellington, near Pontefract, a cross was mistaken for a shepherd's crook and incorporated into a dragon story, with the rather refreshing result that the hero in this case is not a knight but a humble shepherd.

This noble fellow, whose name – Armroyd – sounds like something out of J B Priestley, tackled a fearsome serpent which had the habit of galumphing from the marshy woodlands round about to prey on the flocks tended by shepherd Armroyd and his mates. What a picture this conjures up!

'Ah'm fair fed up o' this', said shepherd Armroyd at the next meeting of Armthorpe branch of the Shepherds' and Foresters' Union.

"Ear, 'ear', cried all the members.

But Armroyd, and he alone, had the courage to tackle the monster, with nothing but his shepherd's crook and his faithful dog. Not surprising, then, that though he slew the dragon, both he and his dog also perished. And that is why a field called Armroyd Close was given to his descendants as a mark of appreciation by his neighbours. Or so they say.

Eccentric Interludes

'What would you call the king if you met him?', I asked my father.

'I'd call him George,' he said.

I felt no need for further questions. If the king were lucky enough to meet my dad, he ought to be properly grateful to him for being so friendly.

Like my father, Jemmy Hirst was a West Riding man and he did meet a king named George – George III. But being Jemmy, he went one better than merely 'calling him George'. He told his majesty that he was glad to find him such a plain old chap and that he'd be welcome any time to visit Jemmy's home at Rawcliffe, there to enjoy all the fine brandy he could sup.

While looking for Jemmy's grave in the churchyard one day I heard a voice behind me: 'Art lookin' for me, lad?' Without even turning round I knew it was Jemmy, which might surprise you, considering the old chap is supposed to have died in 1829. But you see, I have the unnerving knack, often on the most inconvenient occasions, of slipping into a different time-warp.

'By gow', said Jemmy, as he looked me up and down, 'thou cuts a funny figure!'

'No funnier than thee', I retorted. (I know from experience that the best way to handle eccentrics is to give them as good as you get.)

It was clear that he considered himself to be in the height of fashion. He wore his regulation garb of a broad-brimmed hat nine feet around, harlequin breeches, red coat and blue sleeves with a glorious glossy waistcoat of drakes' feathers.

'Do you still go to the races dressed like that?', I asked him.

'Nay', said Jemmy, 'I can't remember when I was last at Doncaster.'

'Is it true that you used to bet with your own banknotes worth fivepence ha'penny each?'

'Aye', said Jemmy. 'I nivver could see why folk made such a fuss about that.'

'They'd make a bigger fuss today', I told him. 'We've gone decimal.'

Jemmy was horrified.

'Ah s'll 'ev to 'ev a word wi' t' king about this. He's not a bad owd chap as I telled 'im when Ah went to court, but Ah'm still waitin' for 'im to coom to Rawcliffe to sample mi brandy.'

I decided not to tell him that there had been quite a few monarchs on the throne since his famous visit to George III. On that celebrated occasion he had travelled to London in his wonderful wickerwork carriage, drawn first by a bull called Jupiter and later by four mules. Jemmy, who could never quite leave well alone, had also fitted the

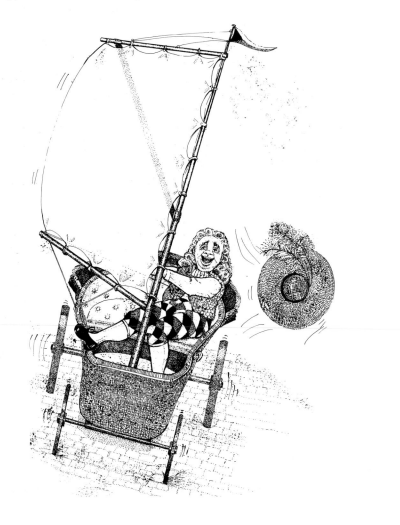

coach with sails. This had disastrous results when he visited Pontefract in his contraption and crashed into a shop window.

''Appen tha'd like a tot', said Jemmy. 'Coom on up to t' 'ouse.'

As we entered the farmyard I was startled to see a handsome bull grazing near the farmhouse door.

'Doan't be freetened', said Jemmy, 'it's nobbut – '

'Jupiter!', I finished for him in amazement.

'Aye', beamed Jemmy, 'that's who it is. 'Appen tha'd like a ride on 'im?'

'An' 'appen not', I said, remembering how, when Jemmy had first ridden him, Jupiter had tossed him over a hedge into a ditch.

''E's as tame as a lamb', smiled Jemmy, as I gave Jupiter a wide berth. 'Just like them pigs.'

Everything on Jemmy's farm apparently lived for ever. The pigs rooting about in the farmyard were clearly the ones he had trained to work as pointers when he went partridge shooting. They ran joyfully to him when he called them by name and were obviously disappointed not to be allowed entry to the house.

And what a house! Instead of curtains, old newspapers covered the windows, while the walls were hung with rusty old farm implements, pots and pans and bicycle wheels.

'Tha'll tak' a glass, tha says? Coom into my coffin! Designed it meself', he added proudly.

Bearing all the marks of a Jemmy Hirst original, it was equipped with folding glass doors and big enough for a small party, which was apparently what he had in mind. He opened a cupboard and produced the brandy bottle, which was a deal emptier when he reluctantly replaced the cork and said, 'Ye'll find your own way out!'

But though I tried everything except breaking the glass of the folding doors, I remained a prisoner in Jemmy Hirst's hospitable coffin, while my host hugged himself and roared with glee.

'It'll cost thee a penny to get out', said Jemmy. 'If tha were a woman it'd cost thee a garter!'

I offered him a penny, 1990s version, and he regarded it with contempt.

'What d'yer call that?'

'It's t' best Ah can do', I told him, 'Pennies aren't what they used to be, an' I'm fresh out o' garters.'

Jemmy grinned. 'I could lend thi a pair', he said.

He pressed a hidden knob to release me from his coffin, then led me to a large, comfortable looking armchair liberally decorated with those items of bygone female attire. But if the chair looked comfortable it was the only thing in that strange dwelling that did.

'When I pop off', said Jemmy, 'we s'll 'ave t' best party they've ever seen i' Rawcliffe. 'Ah'll get t' mayor to declare a public holiday.'

'Tha won't be here', I reminded him.

'No, but it's in mi will,' he retorted. 'An' Ah'm leaving five pund . . . *five pund*,' he repeated, clearly not satisfied with the effect of his first announcement, 'to pay for a bagpiper all t' way from Aberdeen, an' a fiddler to play an' all.'

'Some suitable solemn music, I suppose?'

'Thar't a miserable sort of feller. *Nay!* Ah'll 'ave 'em playin' some reight jolly stuff, like *Ovver the 'Ills an' Far Away*. There'll be all mi racin' pals there, and they'll not want to send me off miserable like', he assured me.

'Ah s'll 'ave t' coffin carried bi eight owd maids. Ah've left a guinea apiece to pay 'em for it. An' if they can't finnd eight owd maids they'll 'ave to mak' do with eight widders − they can have half a crown each.'

I thought of asking him to explain this apparent anomaly but explanations, from Jemmy, might confuse more than they clarified.

'An' that neet, after they've sided me away, there'll be a firework show. By gum it'll be a reight good do − Ah'll fair enjoy lookin' dahn on it all.'

Clearly he had no doubts about his final destination after death, which befell him at the age of ninety-one in October 1829.

But in our time-warp that was still in the future.

'I'm told they call you "the King of Rawcliffe"', I began, but there the interview had to end, for Jemmy raised his hand for silence as he counted the hours the church clock was striking.

'Five o'clock − tea party time!'

He took down a horn from a hook on the wall, carried it to the front door and blew a long, sonorous blast.

Immediately, Rawcliffe was alive with old ladies and children, all skipping or hobbling towards Jemmy's house. He beamed at the sight.

'They'll 'ave a reight good tea, Ah can tell thi', he said. 'An' t' bairns 'll be 'ere tomorrow neet to dance to my fiddlin' − until nine o'clock on the dot. Then Ah ring mi bell an' off they go to bed, prompt!'

Suddenly Jemmy, his house, the children and the old ladies faded from sight and I found myself standing alone in a Rawcliffe much changed from the days when it was Jemmy Hirst's 'kingdom'.

Walton, near Wakefield, is nobbut a cock-stride, as Jemmy might have said, from Rawcliffe. Today, Walton Hall, Squire Waterton's old house, is a conference and leisure centre. It still stands on an island in the middle of a lake, though I doubt if the squire *ever* saw a water-skier skimming the surface as I once did. But there was no-one else there on the day I had yet another of my 'funny turns' and found myself talking to the great man himself.

My first intimation of the presence was a voice from above!

'Hey you, young man, skulking down there, I hope you're not a poacher!'

'Certainly not', I said, looking around frantically for the source of the squeaky old voice.

'You look a bit suspicious to me!'

Suddenly it dawned on me that the owner of the voice could only be high up in one of the many fine trees growing in the park. At last I located him, a man apparently in his eighties standing easily on the bough of a giant oak while he leaned with one hand placed casually against its trunk. All at once he was on the ground beside me, a tall, lean figure, who might have looked austere but for the mischievous twinkle in his eyes.

'This is the only place in England where all animals – especially birds – are free to come and go in safety. I allow nothing to be killed here, sir, except the Hanoverian brown rat, an intruder from the continent, and the enemy, my dear sir, of that poor, injured Briton our native black rat. This park of 260 acres is a refuge for our furred and feathered brothers. Foxes get in of course, being crafty fellows, but even those we never shoot, though they endanger the nesting birds. No sir, I trap them and set them free outside.'

'What year is this?', I asked him.

He gave me a strange look.

'1862, of course.'

'Then this', I told him, 'must be one of the very first bird sanctuaries in the world', whereupon he gave me an even stranger look.

The character of Charles Waterton, born at Walton Hall in 1782, is almost impossible to summarise. Traveller, naturalist, eccentric – he was all of these, as well as a man of almost saintly charity, but it is as a great practical joker and eccentric that we remember him here.

Not that Waterton regarded himself as an eccentric. On the contrary, he was quite indignant at being so described, insisting that he was the most ordinary of men. Even so, two of his better known exploits were capturing an alligator by riding on its back, and climbing to the top of St Peters in Rome, where he left his gloves on the lightning conductor as a calling card. So alarmed was the Pope by this audacious act that he appealed for volunteers to remove the gloves, a task Waterton had to perform himself, since no one else came forward.

'Come inside and look at my specimens', the old boy suddenly invited.

At the front door he pointed to two doorknockers

'Designed 'em miself', he said proudly. 'Which one do you choose?'

Each knocker was in the form of a face, one smiling, the other expressing acute pain. And the 'business end' of each, so to speak, was apparently contrived so as to make its impact on the foreheads above the two faces.

'You've solved it', said the squire in obvious delight when, after hesitating, I chose the knocker above the scowling face and administered a loud rap on the anguished forehead. Treated in such a fashion I'd have done more than grimace!

'Now try the other one', chortled the squire.

But the other knocker refused to move, hence, no doubt, the serenely smiling face beneath it.

Inside the house I saw what the squire called his masterpiece of the taxidermist's art – the Nondescript, which he had once tried to pass off as a new species, a characteristic Waterton joke.

'I was always fond of preserving animals. Made this one out of the skin of a red howler monkey. Some people say I based him on a treasury official I crossed swords with.'

'And did you?', I said.

He smiled.

'I'll tell you this: when I used the Nondescript as the frontispiece of one of my books of travels, some numbskulls actually thought it was me! "What a curious-looking fellow this Waterton must be", they said.'

Was it true, I asked him, that while travelling in Demerara he slept with one big toe protruding from his hammock, hoping to get a vampire bat to bite it?

'Of course', he said. 'I've always been fascinated by that "nocturnal surgeon", as I called the little beast. Can't think why he wouldn't bite me,' he added, sounding aggrieved. 'Perhaps it was because my feet had got so tough from walking barefoot in the jungle.'

I knew enough about Waterton not to ask him about his wife, Anne, the daughter of his friend, Charles Edmonstone. Her death was surely the saddest event of his long and eventful life. He was thirty when they met and she was virtually no age at all, for the occasion was her christening. There and then, as he held her in his arms, Waterton declared his intention some day to marry her. Charles Edmonstone was already dead on the 18th May 1829 when Waterton, now forty-seven, and Anne, a seventeen year old convent girl, were married in the convent chapel in Bruges, where Anne had been living.

When she died in childbirth less than a year later, Waterton embarked on a rigorous life, rising at 3 am and spending much time in prayer in his chapel dedicated to St Catherine of Alexandria, whose portrait, he believed, bore a strong resemblance to his late wife. It was in many ways the life of a recluse.

Suddenly we heard voices from outside and he went to the window.

'Ah, my friends are here,' he said, and a smile I had not seen before lit up his countenance. 'They come from the asylum, you know, and I spend the whole day with them when I can. They picnic in the grounds and I row them on the lake or dance with them. Poor, simple souls, it makes them so happy.'

He bade me a courteous goodbye, told me I could visit his grounds at any time, then strode happily off to welcome his guests, who greeted him with obvious affection. When last I saw his tall, gaunt figure, he was dancing happily hand in hand with two of his asylum visitors.

Not all my interviews ended so happily. But then, Bill Sharp had never really very much to be happy about. He was also an exception in that, throughout the interview, if you can call it that, he was in bed, and that he spoke no more to me than he did to anyone else during all the fifty years he lay there.

All I could remember is finding myself at the door of the farm and being admitted by a brisk, motherly soul who seemed to know more about my business than I did.

'You'll be 'ere to see Mr Sharp', she said. "Is father told me I could let you in. You're favoured, Ah can tell yer. There's not many gets to see 'im, except through 'is little winder. An' then they only see 'im if 'e doesn't see them fust! If they bother him too much he'll hide under the sheets. Coom yer ways in sir', she urged.

'Coom on now, Mr Sharp', she said, addressing a large white-haired figure lying in a bed below the window. 'Ther's a gentleman to see you. Yer must try to be sociable.'

She looked at him with her lips pursed and shook her head as if she doubted that her exhortations would have much effect.

I can picture the scene now, though how I got into such a situation I have not the slightest idea. All I can say is, one moment I had been in the twentieth century and the next I was back in the second half of the nineteenth, sitting in a ground floor room of a farm near Keighley. Through the tiny window I could see a view of desolate moorland. There was a fire in the grate but most of the smoke seemed reluctant to go up the chimney, and when a gust of wind rattled the little window, clouds of it were blown into the room, making me cough.

But the white-haired old man in the bed seemed not to notice it as he lay beneath the sheets with one knee permanently bent through having lain in that position for so long. Indeed, he hardly seemed to notice that I was there and was indifferent, too, when from time to time faces appeared at the window. Men, women, children, sometimes whole families, dressed as if for an afternoon stroll, would take it in turns to peer through at him, grimacing and trying to provoke a reply until he wearied of them and hid beneath the bedclothes.

Bill Sharp was the son of a notorious miser with a bizarre sense of humour whose practical jokes often rebounded on himself. When Bill fell in love with Mary Smith from a neighbouring farm, and the two wanted to wed, Bill's father was too mean to offer a decent marriage settlement, and even though a grandchild was on the way, Mary's father declared that he'd never allow his daughter to marry the son of such a skinflint.

Nevertheless, on the day fixed for the wedding at Keighley Parish Church, Bill duly turned up and waited for his bride . . . and waited. And when at last he realised that Mary would never come to marry him, he went home to his bed – and stayed there.

'He's been there for nigh on fifty year', said Bill's keeper, with a shake of her head. 'I don't reckon he'll ever speak again.'

'He will', I said, before I could restrain myself.

She turned on me sharply. 'How can you know that? What will he say?'

Mercifully the scene faded and I was rescued back into my own century. Otherwise I might have told her that at 4 am on the 3rd March 1856, Bill Sharp would speak, just once, before his death at the age of seventy-nine.

'Poor Bill, poor Bill Sharp,' he would say, five words which summed up the tragi-comedy of his wasted life.

Two Harrys and a Bear

I have met only two of the three characters mentioned in my title –
one of the Harrys, that is, and the bear. All three were famous and,
in a sense, all three were related. Who were they?

If you're half as astute as I think you are, you've already guessed
that the surname of one of my two Harrys is Corbett. From that it's
an easy step to making a not very wild guess that the name of the
bear is Sooty. But what, you ask, is the surname of the other Harry,
the one Harry Corbett called Uncle Harry. Both had strong links with
Guiseley and if you haven't guessed it now, you're no Yorkshireman,
because if Harry Ramsden isn't in my list of famous Tykes, he ought
to be.

Talk about fame . . . How's this for fame? Write a letter to yourself
with no other destination on the envelope than England, and see
how long it takes you to get it. That's what Harry Ramsden did. He
posted his letter in London on the 20th October 1952, and you might
like to guess how long it took that letter, with the head of King
George VI on its 2½d stamp, to get to Guiseley.

Two years? Six months? Wrong again: it was delivered in Guiseley
on October 22nd. And I'm not saying the Postmaster General didn't
give somebody a rocket because it had taken so long! Mind you, after
Harry's name, the envelope did bear the words: 'The Uncrowned
Fish and Chip King'. Not that Harry would ever have made such a
grandiloquent gesture if he hadn't been talked into it by his nephew
Lewis. Harry was far too unassuming to think of such a thing, but he
always enjoyed a good laugh and, surely, no-one laughed louder
than he did when he held that letter in his hand.

Far from giving himself royal airs, Fish and Chip King Harry was
quite likely to be found sweeping the car park outside his 'palace' at
White Cross, Guiseley. And if a customer, failing to recognise him,
tipped him half a crown or even a tanner, saying it was more than
he'd get from 'yon bugger in theer', King Harry would quietly pocket
the tip, smile and carry on with his sweeping.

I wish I'd known him, but I didn't, though I have eaten in King Harry's 'Palace', which was more than he often did himself: he was more likely to be hidden away in a corner somewhere, brooding on the remote possibility of finding a better way to cook fish and chips.

I once went to Harry Ramsden's with a dearly loved friend who, because he had 'a stomach', could be relied upon to make life difficult for the most conscientious and obliging of waitresses. (He was a Lancastrian, of course, so much must be forgiven.) If his food was offered fried, he would politely ask for it grilled. If there was treacle sponge and custard for afters, he would call for rice pudding. The funny thing is, he nearly always got his way.

They would take one look at his innocent Lancashire face, listen to him rolling his Rs in words like Burrrnley and give him the manager on toast if he insisted. But he met his come-uppance on the day we went to Harry Ramsden's and he asked for cod.

The waitress, all smiles until that moment, looked as if she'd been poleaxed with a flounder. Whether it was haddock or plaice or basking shark she'd offered us, I can't remember. What I do remember is my friend saying, with dreadful clarity, and with that funny Lancashire way they have of turning sentences inside out:

'Have you not got cod?'

She staggered, almost dropped the tray with our pot of tea, bread and butter for two on my head, then, faintly but bravely, she said:

'We don't serve cod.'

My friend's trouble was that he never knew when to stop.

'What', he enquired in his innocent Lancashire way, all unaware that he risked being dunked bodily into the chip pan, 'what's wrong with cod?'

That waitress rose to the occasion with a resolution that should have won her a Golden Fish Cake for Conduct Above and Beyond the Call of Funny Lancastrians.

Cod, she explained kindly, was 'all water' and as far as I can remember there the matter was left. The crisis was surmounted and instead of ending his days fried to a golden brown under a mound of chips, my Lancashire friend was graciously permitted to return, unmolested, over the Pennines.

Harry Ramsden didn't inherit his crown from a long line of ancestors, though his dad, yet another Harry, opened a fish and chip shop in Bradford about the turn of the century. Harry meant to reign over his own kingdom, but to do this he needed money. By sheer hard work he was able to start his own taxi business, after driving for another firm, and then, when he was only twenty-one, he took a pub, the Craven Heifer, in Bolton Road, Bradford.

At first business was slow. Harry looked around to see what other, more successful pubs had that the Craven Heifer hadn't. The answer, apparently, was a pianist. Harry hired the best he could find and soon business, like the new pianist, was swinging.

Perhaps that was the moment King Harry first realised the importance of entertaining the customers, or perhaps he had always been a showman at heart. At any rate, his flair for publicity stood him in good stead many times during his career.

After the First World War, during which he served as an Army transport driver in Salonika, Harry opened the first of his own fish and chip shops. Then in 1928 he moved to White Cross, having bought a wooden lock-up shop, the humble forerunner of the present emporium bearing his name, for £150. Unmistakable proof of his success appeared three years later, in 1931, when the biggest fish and chip shop in the world was opened.

We must now move on twenty-one years to bring my other Harry, Harry Corbett, into the picture, though he had been making a name for himself in a very different field for quite a while.

As I've said, Uncle Harry Ramsden had always been a showman at heart, despite his personal modesty, and entertaining seems to have run in the family. So in 1952, when his restaurant reached its twenty-first birthday, he decided to give a party. Nothing very special in that idea. What was special was the fact that Harry Ramsden decided to put the clock back forty years by offering fish and chips at the prices charged by his father at his shop in Manchester Road, Bradford, before the First World War. Fish cost a penny that day in July 1952, and chips a ha'penny. Was it any wonder that the queues stretched for miles? And it surely wasn't so much the Yorkshire nose for a bargain that brought them, as nostalgia.

The party went on far into the night, when fireworks lit up the Guiseley sky, and among those entertaining the customers was Harry Ramsden's nephew, Harry Corbett, whose own success story illustrated at least two attributes the two men had in common – an ability to judge public taste and a willingness to take a risk.

I first interviewed Harry Corbett in 1957, when the television act in which he played the stooge of a teddy bear was well-established. In a way, I was as much a victim of Sooty as Harry often appeared to be. Having two young children who liked nothing better than to see a grown-up squirted with orange juice or brought down to earth in some other way, I had no choice. If they couldn't do it to me (though doubtless they did, on occasions) the next best thing was to do see it done to Harry.

Harry, I remember, seemed slightly embarrassed at being inter-viewed at all. In that, perhaps, he resembled his self-effacing uncle. 'Don't think of me as a desperately mercenary person', he said, soon after we met. He had never really set out to become a TV star or a household name, he explained. 'These things just happen.'

They began happening when Harry, on holiday in Blackpool with his wife Marjorie and two young sons, spotted Sooty, disguised as a glove puppet, in a joke shop on the North Pier. Or it could have been Sooty that spotted Harry, who in all innocence remarked to Marjorie what a sweet little face there was on that mayhem-making bear.

Harry bought the bear, as he thought, to entertain his sons, but anyone who knows Sooty will realise it was only a matter of time before Sooty took over. From that shop window on Blackpool's

North Pier he had recognised Harry as the ideal partner on his way to fame.

One of Harry's qualifications for the job was his prowess as an amateur magician. Here again, this was not something he had really worked at – it 'just happened', at a wartime family party, the sort of event which seemed to be a favourite occupation of the Ramsden-Corbett clan. Harry's younger brother, Leslie, was coming home on leave, so Harry decided to organise an entertainment which included himself as a conjuror. He worked up some card tricks, and, wearing a long cloak and with his face blacked, made his magical debut.

His success at the party, which apparently took him completely by surprise, fired him with enthusiasm, though he still had no notion of swapping his job as an engineer for that of entertainer. He continued to perform purely for fun and was somewhat horrified when one day his grocer announced, 'I've fixed up a show for you, Harry'.

It was useless for him to protest. Fate, or something, a small bear, perhaps, was in control. And so, hardly knowing how it had happened, a very nervous Harry found himself topping the bill at a children's birthday party at the home of his bank manager. Again he was astonished by his success, and even more so when he was offered a fee, which he refused. After much persuasion he reluctantly accepted six packs of playing cards for use in his act.

Sooty, of course, who never missed a trick, especially a card trick, had been watching all this happening and was determined not only to 'get in on the act' but to run it – or should that read *ruin* it. At least that's how it seemed to me when, at my kids' insistence, we watched the two of them on television. Soon Sooty was 'helping' with the card tricks, 'picking a card' at Harry's invitation and somehow always managing to leave Harry with egg on his face, quite often literally.

But in those days Harry still had no notion of becoming a pro, though he was now appearing all over Yorkshire at parties. And everywhere that Harry went, the bear was sure to go, and everybody told them: 'You ought to be on TV'. For years Harry merely laughed at that. Then he began to wonder . . .

Guiseley had a village atmosphere in those days – it still has. Everybody seemed to know everyone else, so naturally Harry Corbett knew Barney Colehan, the BBC producer whose name will forever be linked with the televising of old time music hall from the City Varieties in Leeds.

'Any chance of Sooty on TV, Barney?', said Harry.

'I might be able to get you an amateur spot on closed-circuit TV at the Radio Exhibition in Manchester', said Barney.

But even this small chance seemed to have proved too good to be true when Barney rang Harry to tell him the programme was now fixed and final and there was no room for additional acts.

Then, as in all the best success stories, the unexpected happened. Someone 'dropped out' and Harry was offered an interview in Manchester at such short notice that he hadn't even time to ask for a day off – he just took it and went off to do an audition. A top producer was watching the shows to choose the best items from the past three or four weeks for a live show of amateurs.

Harry had hardly finished before the visiting producer said: 'I want that bear in tomorrow night'.

The man from Guiseley who had begun entertaining at a family party must have felt that things were getting rather out of hand: he was not used to such high-powered stuff, but the producer wouldn't be thwarted, even though it meant cutting one minute from each of the other performances. Somehow or other, Harry would just have to condense his turn into four minutes.

It seemed he had no choice. Fate (or Sooty) had taken over and there seemed to be just nothing he could do about it – except feel nervous! That is, until the effervescent anchor man Macdonald Hobley, who was introducing the artists, saw Sooty and had a fit of the giggles. Harry relaxed immediately and the result was a triumph. Everybody, from the call boy to the managing director, seemed to be assuring him that his future on television was assured.

Eric Fawcett, the producer who'd picked Harry and Sooty for their best-of-the-series appearance, advised him to change Sooty's appearance to his own design and register him as a copyright trade design. All Harry had to do, it seemed, was wait for his success to fulfil all its promises.

For weeks he waited. He must have begun to wonder if it had all been a flash in the pan when he got a note from the head of BBC Children's Television asking him to go for an interview. He was offered six fortnightly six-minute shows on *Saturday Special* at ten guineas a time, which, although it bought a great deal more than it does today, was hardly enough to make him throw up a steady job with a good pension – not without some serious thinking and a good deal of discussion with Marjorie.

If he could only carry on with his engineering job at Guiseley until Sooty was really established . . . Harry asked his employers for time off to do the series and suggested they took it off his holidays.

'Sorry, Harry,' they said, 'we'd like to keep you, but you have to choose – it's got to be either TV or engineering.'

He was enough of a realist to see their point of view. His career, he realised, was at the crossroads. Which way should he take?

It was Marjorie who helped to make his mind up. She knew where his heart was leading him, and in spite of the obvious risks, she had no intention, she said, of ending her days in the company of a disappointed 'crabby old man'!

So he accepted the offer of that first series and of the series that followed. Then Chad Valley, the toy people, approached him with an offer – they wanted to manufacture a Sooty puppet. Harry agreed, and another milestone had been passed.

Success followed success. Sooty made a triumphant appearance on Vic Oliver's programme *This is Show Business*, which prompted his old Guiseley friend Barney Colehan to suggest a 'one-off' adult show called *Sooty Stays Up*. Success again! It seemed Sooty couldn't put a paw wrong. But when another adult show produced even higher viewing figures and the possibility was mooted of a Sooty series for adults, Harry's native common sense warned him to think twice before accepting the unquestionably attractive offer. Adults, he knew, got fed up eventually of even the most popular act if they saw too much of it, but there was always a new generation of children coming up, to whom Sooty's antics would be fresh and new.

One thing about Sooty – stardom may go to his head now and then when he appears in the West End or makes a film, but he certainly wears well. But then, why should he show his age? He's magic, isn't he? And that's one of the reasons his fans not only love but envy him.

I saw letters from five and six year olds asking why he goes to bed without pyjamas, and others, more urgent, complaining that the writers' wands won't work. Or asking to borrow Sooty's, 'because I do not like school much and I want to magic myself into a man'. Generally, however, it is the anarchist in Sooty that they adore: 'I love him when he hits hary corbut on the head and slaps him on the face with a cipper and sqirts woter on his face with a pistol and messes his suute up with eggs and I am hoping that you would tell me if Sooty was a pupit or not'. Good question.

Harry died very peacefully in his sleep in 1989 at the age of seventy-one, and it seems right and proper that his son Matthew should have taken over where his dad left off. After all, it was to amuse Matthew that Harry first bought Sooty's original in 1948.

That bear may be an international star these days, but having left Blackpool for Guiseley all those years ago, he's now very much a Yorkshire bear at heart. If you doubt that, you need only go to Windhill Manor on the Leeds road in Shipley and enter Sooty's World for yourself. Here, in a video theatre, Harry himself relives for delighted present-day kids those early episodes in which Sooty works his magical mischief.

Here, too, you can discover just what a versatile bear this is as you see Sooty working out in his personal gym, operating in his hospital, presiding as a judge in his own courtroom or running his circus. You can even see him officiating in his very own fish and chip shop . . . Uncle Harry Ramsden would have been pleased about that.

Comical Customs

There is in these Broad Acres a kind of inspired lunacy which surfaces at intervals quite unrelated to the phases of the moon (or 'mooin'). These periods may be recognised by such manifestations as the World Coal-Carrying Championship at Gawthorpe, and by others hereinafter described.

To all intents and purposes, Gawthorpe is a perfectly harmless little place near Ossett (a slightly bigger place but equally harmless). You may not believe it, but many people in the British Isles don't even know Gawthorpe or Ossett exist, and would never dream of visiting them. What a mistake!

Let them nobbut set foot in Gawthorpe on Easter Monday and they'll know exactly what I mean about the uniqueness of Yorkshire. In this village a contest which attracts rather more enthusiasm locally than the Olympic Games is held to decide who is the King of the Coal Humpers. And since, even in Gawthorpe these days, the so-called fairer sex can't let the men keep owt to themselves, they have to find a coal Humpers' Queen, too.

Did I call them the fairer sex? If they're all that fair, how do they get away with carrying a 20 kilo bag of coal ('coil', that is) when the fellas have to carry 50? Furthermore, the women need only trip lightly from t' bottom o' t' village to the maypole on Gawthorpe's village green, whereas the chaps have to start way back at the Royal Oak in Owl Lane, which means they have to run 1,012.5 metres (that's the best part of a mile in English).

If the relative distances between these starting and finishing points convey nothing to you, don't blame me – it just means you've never travelled. You'll be telling me next you didn't know Gawthorpe had a maypole. But don't let them hear you saying that in Gawthorpe, because that maypole is undoubtedly their proudest possession.

Pitched battles have been fought over it in the past, chiefly against the inhabitants of neighbouring Streetside. Jealous of so proud a

totem, the 'Streetsiders' pinched it on at least one occasion. It has stood on the village green since at least 1875. And if Gawthorpe has owt to do with it, it'll stand there forever, because Gawthorpe folk doubtless believe it embodies the luck of the whole community.

Every year, on the first Saturday in May, Gawthorpe holds its maypole celebrations, when the longest procession you've ever seen marches to Ossett and back, complete with bands, a May queen, all kinds of famous antiquated vehicles and other excitements too numerous to list. (It may well be that this exercise is really a show of strength to deter any of Gawthorpe's neighbours who might fancy their chances at kidnapping that overgrown barber's pole again, around which the maypole dancing team will in due course present a programme of intricate terpsichore, or fancy dancin'.)

But we were talking about coal-carrying. How, you might ask, did such a remarkable custom originate?

Believe it or not, it all comes back to that maypole, which provides a sort of focus for village activities, especially those of a charitable kind. Charity, indeed, is the *raison d'être*, as they might say in Ossett, of the maypole committee itself, that august body which first decided that a coal-carrying contest was just the thing to raise funds for good causes. (They'd considered a rolling pin-throwing event, but some of the menfolk feared the women might be too practised at that already, thus gaining an unfair advantage.)

The coal-carrying race officially lasts four and a half minutes, and record-holders have appeared in the Guinness Book of Records. There are modest cash prizes and commemorative trophies, plus other rewards, the nature of which depends on who is sponsoring the event. But as they'll tell you in Gawthorpe, it's the honour of winning, not the prizes, that has attracted entrants from America and, who knows, perhaps even Ossett.

This laudable lunacy of Yorkshire folk takes a different and rather more credible form at Denby Dale, not far from Huddersfield, where every so often they make a giant pie. They then invite gastronomes (or expert eyters) from the whole of Yorkshire – and from outer space itself if there's a bus running – to help them eat it.

Here again, the object of the exercise is the laudable one of raising brass, whether to help a local hospital or to build a village hall, which is what they did with the proceeds of the pie of 1964 – 'the world's biggest pie', as they confidently called the six ton monster into which went 10 bullocks, 1½ tons of spuds, 5 hundredweight of lard and 50 gallons of gravy.

The first Denby Dale Pie, so far as we know, was made in 1788 to celebrate the recovery of King George III from mental illness. They also made a pie to mark Wellington's victory at Waterloo. They made one in honour of the repeal of the Corn Laws, and in 1887 they made the pie they would remember when all the rest had been forgotten. It was so big that a four-wheeled cart and two horses were needed to pull it, though the size of it only made matters worse. Why? Because it went bad – and how!

What was to be done with a pie that no-one could eat?

'Nowt! Nobbut bury it', somebody must have said.

'Aye', someone else agreed, 'but we mun give it a proper funeral.'

'What a good idea!' said everybody at once, agreeing that this would be almost as much fun as having a pie they could eat.

So the local laureate composed a poem beginning:

'Strong, strong was the smell
that compelled us to part,

From a treat to our stomachs,
A salve to our hearts.'

And a funeral card was printed 'in affectionate remembrance of the Denby Dale Pie which died August 27th 1887, aged three days'.

They buried it in quicklime in Toby Wood, where, they say, if the wind is in the right (or wrong) direction, its fragrance lingers still.

You can't keep a bad pie down, it seems, even if you bury it, for on the funeral card just quoted there is a footnote announcing 'THE RESURRECTION PIE . . . This has been made by the ladies of the village and is expected to be a success' (unlike its disastrous predecessor whose making had been rashly entrusted to cooks from London).

It's traditional in Denby Dale to make each pie bigger than the one before, but admirable as such ambition may be, it has its dangers. Twice – in 1928 and in 1964 – the pie got stuck in t' oven!

Kilburn in North Yorkshire makes no bones, or even pie-crust, about the nature of its own great comic event, held in July. The Kilburn Feast and Local Costume Frolics they call this event, as if to warn visitors that they'd better turn up in the right frolicking spirit or they might find themselves fined as much as twenty pence by the 'Mayor' for something as apparently innocent as having a nodding dog in the car's rear window. The 'Mayor's' term of office may only last for 'a year and a day', but on the day of the frolics he is virtually omnipotent.

He is accompanied in the mayoral 'coach' (a trap drawn by a local lad) by the 'Mayoress', whose stylish garb deceives no-one. 'She' is as much a man as her consort and privileged to kiss any girl 'she' fancies – all in the cause of charity, of course.

Once you've been involved, even as an innocent bystander, in these carryings-on, you'll understand why Kilburn has been called 'a village of schoolboys'.

What else but a village of schoolboys would have embarked on the creation of its own white horse, just because a native of Kilburn, visiting the famous prehistoric white horse at Uffington in Oxfordshire, thought that Kilburn should have one too.

Thomas Taylor was his name and he had done very nicely, thank you, by selling Yorkshire hams and bacon to Londoners, who appreciated them mightily, the poor things, having nothing half so ambrosial in the capital.

But despite his success, the local-boy-made-rich never forgot his native village. He wrote to the local schoolmaster, John Hodgson, who, as luck would have it, was a surveyor in his spare time, and therefore just the man to help in such a project. John Hodgson appears to have been a teacher somewhat in advance of his age, and certainly one whose horizons were not limited by the three Rs.

Having somehow decided that Kilburn's white horse was to occupy a site on a nearby cliff, Roulston Scar, he turned Operation White Horse into an exercise for his pupils, setting them the task of marking out the outline of the steed: it was to be 314 feet long and 228 feet high. (And just to give you an idea of the size of this animal, I've seen it stated, though not demonstrated, that thirty people can stand on its eye alone.)

About thirty men of the village cut out the shape of the horse from the hillside turf, coated it with lime and then, no doubt, had a jolly good frolic to celebrate.

Alas for good intentions! Unlike the chalk which provides a base for the prehistoric white horse of Uffington, the friable surface of Roulston Scar offered no resistance to the elements and from the moment of its horse's making, Kilburn became engaged in an unending battle to keep it white. All manner of means have been employed – lime, chalk chippings set in lime, and even spent carbide. Every so often, for one reason or another, the White Horse of Kilburn finds its way into the news. If nothing else, it is a unifying factor for Kilburn and certainly a fine publicity gimmick.

Not that Kilburn needs one. For all sorts of reasons it is one of the best known villages in Yorkshire. It was, after all, the home of 'the Mouse Man', woodcarver Bob Thompson, whose 'trademark', a mouse, is to be found on fine furniture in many parts of Britain, but most noticeably, I think, in Yorkshire.

And where better could anybody, mouse or man, wish to be found?

A Haunted Man

My bookcase is haunted. I only discovered this the other day, though I've known for some time that, as my Uncle Ephraim might say, there's summat varry peculiar about it. For one thing, I can never find in it any book I'm actually looking for at the time. I search the thing methodically and finally conclude: *(a)* that some fanatical collector of decaying volumes has stolen it; *(b)* it's been destroyed by a kind of spontaneous combustion, very rare in books; *(c)* it's been eaten by the cat – our cat's like that; or *(d)*, which is of course completely inconceivable, I've absent-mindedly mislaid it.

My wife, if questioned (and probably even if not consulted at all), would be the first to tell you that *(d)* is by far the most likely. When I've lost my glasses she always knows as if by instinct that they'll turn up in the most unlikely place. Since I know myself to be almost obsessionally careful where I put things, I can only conclude that my glasses are haunted too. If so, she, of all people, should be able to tell me, because she is undoubtedly psychic.

'What have you lost now?', she'll say, in an infuriatingly matter-of-fact voice, before I've even said I've lost anything.

I have in fact gone to great lengths to avoid giving that impression, walking casually about the house, hands in pockets, now and then dropping to my hands and knees to look under the sofa to see how the carpet is wearing. Or whistling airily as I tip out the contents of the dustbin on the lawn on the pretext that it's good for the grass. So how can she know?

Yet somehow she always does. The really galling thing is that she treats me as if I were the sort of person who can actually be expected to lose things.

I fix her with a piercing gaze.

'What makes you think I've lost anything?', I ask in my best QC style, adjusting an imaginary gown.

'I know you', she replies, completely unintimidated.

But that, as I know now, is where she's wrong! The truth is that not only my bookcase, but my glasses and, oh, lots of other items of my daily life, are haunted. It's the only possible reason why, for instance, my dirty socks should regularly appear in the breadbin.

'You see before you', I shall say, 'a haunted man!'

Or I would – if I didn't know perfectly well that she'd come back at me with some quite unjustified but unanswerable riposte.

The trouble is that like so many other people who are overflowing with common sense, she's got a closed mind. People like her are a great thorn in the flesh of sensitive souls like me, whose lives are subject to intervention from forces in the Great Unknown. People, for instance, like a former caretaker at York's Museum Library.

One Sunday evening in September 1953, being apparently alone in the building, he was making a security check when, to his surprise, he heard footsteps and on further investigation found a stranger searching the curator's office.

Asked his business, the stranger, dressed 'like a professor', in frock coat and drainpipe trousers, made no reply. But as the caretaker followed him out of the room and into the library, he was heard muttering, 'I must find it, I must find it', as if to himself. Next he began rummaging among the books on one of the shelves.

Perhaps the stranger was deaf. He certainly made no response when the caretaker offered to escort him to the curator's home. To attract his attention, the caretaker touched him on the shoulder, whereupon the mysterious visitant vanished, dropping on the floor a book that a moment before he had held in his hand. Its title: *Antiquities and Curiosities of the Church.*

Next morning the caretaker told the curator what had happened and showed him the book, still lying on the floor where it had fallen. What the curator made of it is not recorded, nor how he reacted when, four weeks later, the incident was repeated. This time the caretaker saw the old man enter the library apparently through locked doors and simply 'fade away' through other doors on his way out. A further four weeks later, the caretaker, with a friend as witness, saw yet another repetition.

Beginning to doubt his senses, perhaps, the caretaker consulted his doctor, who was sufficiently intrigued to make one of the party of six who four weeks later waited, on an evening in December 1953, for a further apparition. The others included the caretaker and his brother, a solicitor and a local journalist. This time no spectre

appeared, but at 7.42 pm, two minutes earlier than on previous occasions, a rubbing sound was heard as the same book was slowly withdrawn from its place on the shelf and dropped on the floor, where it remained upright.

And that, apart from the doctor complaining that his legs had felt decidedly chilly up to the knees, was all that happened; nor did anything more occur the following February, when a dozen would-be witnesses, including members of the Society for Psychical Research, waited in the library, seeing nothing but experiencing the aforementioned cold knees (cold feet too, perhaps).

Maybe the 'ghost' was publicity-shy or merely unco-operative. At any rate, no more sightings were reported, at least to my knowledge. But for some time speculation continued. If there were a ghost, *whose* ghost? Some believed it might be that of a Darlington solicitor and antiquary, dead then for some thirty years, who had once owned the book which figured in the appearances. But only the ghost knows for certain, and so far he hasn't told me. You could try consulting my wife. . .

At this point the more sceptical among my readers might say scornfully, 'Is that it then? Is that what you call being a haunted man?' Such doubters will be answered with a hollow laugh and the words *'Would that it were!'*, spoken in an echoing voice that will freeze their blood . . . because, dear sceptical reader, I haven't told you the half of it yet (a third, perhaps, but no more). There is, for example, the case of the vanishing bedclothes. . .

An historical example of this is associated with Bolling Hall, Bradford, an old manor house, which is now a much-visited museum. During the Civil War the house was owned by Richard Tempest, who was a Royalist, unlike the vast majority in Bradford who were Puritans and supported Cromwell against King Charles I.

It was hardly surprising, then, that Bradford was in great disfavour with the Royalists and after the Royalist Earl of Newcastle established his headquarters at Bolling Hall, the city was threatened with a massacre which would spare no-one, man, woman or child. In fact, the earl had issued the order 'No quarter' before going to bed . . . but not to sleep – thanks to the Bolling Hall ghost.

All through the night, we're told, a spectral female figure in white persisted in pulling the bedclothes from the earl's bed and wailing 'Pity poor Bradford!' Whether it was really a disguised member of the Bradford Roundhead and Parliamentarian Amateur Thespian Society, who took it upon herself to save the city, has never been revealed, but whoever it was, it did the trick. Bradford was spared.

On reflection, it couldn't have been a local stage star, or we'd have known: after the armistice she'd have made jolly sure the story got front page billing in the *Telegraph and Argus* – probably by pulling the sheets off the editor's bed until he agreed.

What I want to know is, who is the secret messenger who pulls the sheets off *my* bed? My home town is not under siege and I am not in a position to spare anybody, but it's perfectly clear that *somebody* wants something from me or I wouldn't keep waking up night after night with cold feet (a well known accompaniment of psychic manifestations). I do wish it'd make up its mind what it wants. Since my wife denies all knowledge of the occurrence, I can only repeat my conviction that I am indeed a haunted man.

Here is one last example, which is probably all your shattered nerves can stand. Every night before I go to bed I meticulously switch off the lights, make sure every tap is turned off, let in the cat and put out the empty milk bottles. Finally I make sure that the slot in the letterbox is unimpeded so that tidings of any bequests from forgotten relatives reach me unhindered.

Why, then, do I find on waking that some mysterious agency has either turned on the lights or the radio or stuffed the cat halfway into the letterbox? I don't advise you to consult my wife: her response, as usual, would be predictable and dismissive of any suggestion of supernatural intervention. But only the other day I found a case so closely echoing my own that it proves I am indeed as haunted as I say I am.

The incident took place some twenty years ago at a club in Bradford. Ironically enough, the purely human participant was a former policewoman, a teacher of judo, who would doubtless have taken in charge any run-of-the-mill prankster.

After staying behind to talk to friends, she was late leaving the club, and it was five minutes past midnight when she decided to visit the ladies' powder room. Having opened the first door and entered a lobby area, she was about to open the second door when she was startled to see the motionless figure of a grey-haired man with glassy staring eyes. He was wearing a dark suit which appeared to be wet.

She tried with all her might to open the door, but it remained firmly shut. Furthermore, when she placed her hand on the long handle of the door she found, beneath her own hand, another, cold as ice — with four fingers, but no thumb!

'Move, for God's sake', she screamed at the figure, but neither it nor the door would budge.

She cried out for help and to her heart-felt relief the door was at last rammed open and she was pulled to safety. Even so, her jumper was seen by her rescuers to stretch as though something or somebody was trying to hold her back. She remembered no more, because at that point she fainted.

The cleaners at the club were in no doubt that the cause of the incident was 'Fred', their name for a figure which had been seen crossing the stage or sitting on steps, head in hands, or whose chill, invisible presence was sometimes sensed as a brooding onlooker.

But who was Fred and what was his purpose? Older residents of that area of Bradford thought they knew. The club, they said, stood on the site of a dyehouse and mill dam, where, many years before, an engineer had been accidentally drowned – a man who was known to have lost the thumb of one hand.

Precisely why Fred should choose to return to the scenes of his earthly life we don't know, but he certainly had ways of making his presence felt. One was to switch lights on and off – some witnesses even claimed to have seen the switch button move apparently of its own volition, and that's the bit that interests me. Because if I could actually show my wife the switch being operated by some invisible spectral hand, I might be able to stop her insisting that the lights are on simply because I left 'em on!

But I must admit that I doubt it. In any case, at our house these phenomena only occur at night. I'd have to keep her standing there watching the light switch while I held a torch to make sure she saw it move. I can't see her agreeing to that – she's too fond of her bed to go in for ghostly witch-swatching, or even switch-watching. Even if, due to all this worry, I popped off first and came back to haunt her she'd never believe it. Seems like the only thing haunted at our house will have to be me – and my bookcase, my glasses, and a few other odds and ends.

Good at Acting Daft

'He's good at acting daft, as we say in Yorkshire.'

Until I heard that said the other day, I didn't even know we did say such a thing – even in Yorkshire. Not as a regular thing that is. But 'daft as it sounds' (and that's summat we do say here), the simple saying quoted at the head of this chapter contains a wealth of wisdom. To be good at acting daft is to appear simple, or even downright half-witted, when it suits you. 'Acting daft' goes hand in hand with 'keepin' yer face straight', an art that was practised in Yorkshire long before the Americans invented the expression 'deadpan'.

Some of the best-known Yorkshire jokes are perfect examples of what I mean. Take the supposed rural simpleton, asked the way to Skipton by a visiting toff who wound his car window down in Burnsall. The local knew the answer well enough, but advised the enquirer that if *he* were going to Skipton he 'wouldn't start from here'. Suspecting that his leg was being pulled, the bigwig demanded: 'Do you know who I am, my good man?'

No, said the local, who confessed, on further questioning, that he didn't know the time, or even what day it was.

'What do you know?' exploded the bigwig.

A beatific smile spread over the local's visage.

'Ah knaw A'h'm not lost', he said.

He knew he wasn't daft, either, good though he might be at appearing so. But because we're so good at acting daft in Yorkshire, we sometimes give a wrong impression.

Rabbie Burns was not a Yorkshireman, but he kenned this truth as weel as onny: it's all a matter of the difference between appearance and reality. 'O wad some Pow'r the giftie gie us to see oursels as others see us!', said Burns. Had he been a Yorkshireman and able to talk proper like the rest of us, he might have said: 'It 'ud be a reight good job if folk could nobbut see theirsens t'same road as other folk sees 'em'. But then, nobody's perfect and what can you expect of people that call haggis 'great chieftain o' the puddin'-race', as if they'd never heard of Barnsley black pudding.

All of which is nobbut a lead-in, as you might say, to a few profound remarks on the difference between the Yorkshireman as he sees himself and the utterly fallacious ideas cherished by folk less fortunate. And when I refer to 'Yorkshiremen', I'm not forgetting Yorkshirewomen (as if they'd let you). Indeed, throughout this book I shall adhere to the long-held belief that there's a difference between the two. *Vive la difference*, or, as we say in Yorkshire, a reight good job an' all!

But to return to my theme: how *is* the Yorkshireman seen by the Others? For years attitudes towards us have ranged from patronage through indifference to bitter hatred. (Most of these your Yorkshireman confronts with a lofty tolerance that refuses to be either pitied or bullied.) Latterly, however, I've noticed a tendency on the part of smart radio and TV discussion programmes to include a token Yorkshireman whose utterances are greeted with a kind of respectful bewilderment.

For instance, in the middle of a learned discussion on bathing habits (you know the sort of thing: Did Nero invent the jacuzzi?) the Yorkshire guest, anxious to do his share, might venture along these lines:

'Ah allus remember t' way mi mother wod grab us when we came in mucky an' chuck us fully cloathed into t' set-pot – mi dad an' all, in 'is pit muck.'

If this doesn't give the chairman a stroke, it will certainly cause the engineers to close down the transmitter in the belief that the Martians have landed.

Very few producers can cope with this kind of stress, so one of two things happens: either they get rid of all this dazzling Yorkshire wit as soon as possible, or they manifest their acute sense of inferiority by turning into pseudo-Yorkshiremen and inventing Yorkshire backgrounds, parents and, worst of all, accents, for themselves. The urbane anchor-man, who has never been further north than St Albans, is inclined to wind up the programme thus:

'Well – er – lads and lasses, Ah reckon we've had a reight good do. By gum we have an' all, an' my thanks are due (tha what? Not arf!). An' my thanks are (is? are?) due to all who've partici – parti – takken part i' t' job. 'Appen you'll tune in for some more intellectual 'omely fun next week, like, when our guest will be Mrs Annie Flatherswaite of Cleckheckmonsedge . . . 'Appen – er – nobbut.'

Far from deploring this respectful lack of comprehension, we should encourage it, because the less they understand us, the more we have them at a disadvantage. We ourselves know that we are of all men the mildest, slow to anger and as full of brotherly love as a Scot is of whisky or a Geordie of what he insists on calling Newcastle Broon Ale. Paradoxically, it may be the simple warmth of our nature that creates the illusion that we are dangerously unpredictable, while our straight-faced humour makes them uncertain whether we're all Einsteins or nobbut ninepence in t' shillin'.

To be honest, this confusion may have been generated by some of our customs, which at first sight do appear rather strange. And for sheer daftness, some might say, the Penny Hedge ceremony at Whitby takes some beating. Canon Atkinson, the renowned Cleveland historian, not a man to mince his words, called it 'a farcical, objectless ceremony', and what would *you* call building a hedge that keeps nowt in and nowt out, for the sole purpose of letting the tide knock it down?

Imagine the impression made on morning strollers past Whitby's upper harbour on the eve of Ascension Day (a movable feast that usually falls in May). Three men wearing gumboots and determined expressions, carrying what look like pea-sticks and a horn that might have once belonged to Robin Hood, squelch across the harbour mud. The hornblower looks on as the other two hammer stakes into the mud, then weave the twigs around them to make a rough fence.

Then the hornblower solemnly raises his horn to his lips and rouses the early snoozers with a piercing blast.

'Out on ye, out on ye, out on ye', he pronounces, then the three retrace their steps across the harbour mud to the harbourside and the onlookers wonder what it's all been about.

The custom is said to have been imposed by the Abbot of Whitby as a penance on three hunters who slew a hermit in whose cell a wild boar had taken refuge, but for centuries historians, like the sea, have poured cold water over the whole affair.

I am not for a moment suggesting that the Penny Hedge protagonists are in anything but deadly earnest; and if some fearful unknown fate might befall us without their intervention, they'd better keep it up. Keep it up anyway – why not? At least it helps to confuse visiting strangers and gives the rest of us summat to argue about.

Not so serious, perhaps, in their performance are the Pace Eggers of the Hebden Bridge area. Characters including St George, Slasher, the Doctor and the Black Morocco Prince, wearing colourful smocks and flower-trimmed hats and brandishing wooden swords, strut and fume, battle and boast, die and are resuscitated with enormous gusto.

They do it now for charity, but their ancestors would beg at the houses and farms in the district for 'money, sweet eggs and strong beer' as they sang a traditional Pace Egg song. This is not the place to delve into the history and symbolism of the play, which features in this book simply as an example of Yorkshire fun and games and of that apparent light-hearted idiocy which proves, if proof were needed, just how good we are at 'acting daft'.

Before we had the variable delights of the telly, even before folk joyfully made fools of themselves in Sunday school concerts and working men's club talent contests, before the Hippodromes and Empires of the music hall era provided light relief in the drably heroic lives of the 'working class', the Pace Eggers would claim their open-air stage in Pennine towns and villages.

And it's good that, amid much boasting and swashbuckling, they still do. St. George and Bold Slasher still fight. Slasher is invariably wounded, but the Doctor unfailingly restores him to health. Indeed, for a practitioner with his qualifications, the case presents few difficulties. As he tells us himself, he can cure:

> 'The itch, the stitch, the palsy and the gout.
> If a man has nineteen devils in his soul,
> I can cast twenty of them out.'

Simple stuff, perhaps, but what it might lack in subtlety is made up for in the bravura of the players, a style which seems to come naturally to the youngsters who, to this day, perform these plays before fascinated crowds.

However, any off-comed-un wishing to prove once and for all that Yorkshire is inhabited by amiable loonies might do worse than visit Ilkley on the occasion of the Black Hats versus White Hats cricket match. He might find it hard to believe that this elegant town, with a history predating the Romans (who named it Olicana), and which found fame and prosperity as the Victorian 'Spa amid the Heather'; a town whose literature festival and other artistic ventures bring performers and audiences from far and wide, could permit such a game within its boundaries.

But then, as a comer-in, he might not understand that a passion for Pushkin or a mania for Mendelssohn can co-exist with a game whose rules exist to be broken and where any 'excess of zeal and aptitude' is solemnly penalised . . . On the other hand, recalling that Ilkley Moor is the birthplace of Yorkshire's tribal dirge, he might realise that, in Yorkshire, anything can happen.

Incidentally, after the very first match, played under skies as black as anyone's hat in September 1880, one spectator did indeed cop 'is deeath o' cowd. The players, it was said, had to listen for the ball that day, because they were unable to see it. We can only hope and trust the old lad died happy.

I've never played for the White Hats or the Black Hats, though in view of the topsy-turvy nature of the game I ought to be a natural for it. When, inevitably, I was out first ball, I could argue that under the eccentric rules the bowler had in fact disposed not of me but of the captain of the opposing side.

It's a pity such a code did not apply at my old school, where the rules seemed always to be weighted against me, in work or at play. My trophies were few and far between. As a 'Mixed Infant' I was awarded, thanks entirely to my mother's efforts, a Clean Hands certificate, one of many supplied to the school, by Lifebuoy I think. She later tore it up in disgust, saying I had failed to live up to it. I can't recall that I've ever missed it overmuch.

Later in life I derived more pleasure from a letter and certificate all the way from America which announced that in recognition of my humble efforts at being funny on paper I'd been made 'a Knight of Mark Twain'. Since that was the only knighthood I'm likely to receive, at least a week passed before I lost it.

Just when I lost another prized certificate I can't quite remember, but I know that it said I had 'passed all the necessary examinations and duly qualified as a member of the above Fraternity' – that fraternity being the Henpecked Club. As I've explained elsewhere in this book, this confirmed my mother-in-law's worst fears about my fitness to be her daughter's husband.

Perhaps it merely proved that I am incurably a Yorkshireman and therefore 'good at acting daft' (a bit too good at times, perhaps). To those who might opine, 'Aye, well, he's niver been much good at owt else', I would simply reply, 'Ah'd rayther act daft than *be* daft'. And to those who can recognise the difference, I affectionately dedicate this book.

AMERICAN ACA
OF OPHTHALMOL

Lens and Cataract

Last major revision 2016–2017

2018-2019
BCSC
Basic and Clinical Science Course™

Protecting Sight. Empowering Lives.®

The American Academy of Ophthalmology is accredited by the Accreditation Council for Continuing Medical Education (ACCME) to provide continuing medical education for physicians.

The American Academy of Ophthalmology designates this enduring material for a maximum of 10 *AMA PRA Category 1 Credits*™. Physicians should claim only the credit commensurate with the extent of their participation in the activity.

CME expiration date: June 1, 2019. *AMA PRA Category 1 Credits*™ may be claimed only once between June 1, 2016, and the expiration date.

BCSC® volumes are designed to increase the physician's ophthalmic knowledge through study and review. Users of this activity are encouraged to read the text and then answer the study questions provided at the back of the book.

To claim *AMA PRA Category 1 Credits*™ upon completion of this activity, learners must demonstrate appropriate knowledge and participation in the activity by taking the posttest for Section 11 and achieving a score of 80% or higher. For further details, please see the instructions for requesting CME credit at the back of the book.

The Academy provides this material for educational purposes only. It is not intended to represent the only or best method or procedure in every case, nor to replace a physician's own judgment or give specific advice for case management. Including all indications, contraindications, side effects, and alternative agents for each drug or treatment is beyond the scope of this material. All information and recommendations should be verified, prior to use, with current information included in the manufacturers' package inserts or other independent sources, and considered in light of the patient's condition and history. Reference to certain drugs, instruments, and other products in this course is made for illustrative purposes only and is not intended to constitute an endorsement of such. Some material may include information on applications that are not considered community standard, that reflect indications not included in approved FDA labeling, or that are approved for use only in restricted research settings. **The FDA has stated that it is the responsibility of the physician to determine the FDA status of each drug or device he or she wishes to use, and to use them with appropriate, informed patient consent in compliance with applicable law.** The Academy specifically disclaims any and all liability for injury or other damages of any kind, from negligence or otherwise, for any and all claims that may arise from the use of any recommendations or other information contained herein.

AAO, AAOE, American Academy of Ophthalmology, Basic and Clinical Science Course, BCSC, EyeCare America, EyeNet, EyeSmart, EyeWiki, Femtocenter, Focal Points, IRIS, ISRS, OKAP, ONE, Ophthalmic Technology Assessments, *Ophthalmology, Ophthalmology Retina*, Preferred Practice Pattern, ProVision, The Ophthalmic News & Education Network, and the AAO logo (shown on cover) and tagline (Protecting Sight. Empowering Lives.) are, among other marks, the registered trademarks and trademarks of the American Academy of Ophthalmology.

Cover image: From BCSC Section 12, *Retina and Vitreous.* End-stage chorioretinal atrophy in pathologic myopia. *(Courtesy of Richard F. Spaide, MD.)*

MIX
Paper from responsible sources
FSC www.fsc.org FSC® C103061

Printed in the United States of America.